Writer's Workshop for the Common Core

Warren E. Combs, Ph.D.

EYE ON EDUCATION
6 DEPOT WAY WEST, SUITE 106
LARCHMONT, NY 10538
(914) 833–0551
(914) 833–0761 fax
www.eyeoneducation.com

Library of Congress Cataloging-in-Publication Data

Combs, Warren E.
  Writer's workshop for the common core : a step-by-step guide / Warren E. Combs.
      p. cm.
  ISBN 978-1-59667-192-8
  1. English language—Composition and exercises—Study and teaching
(Elementary)   2. Writers' workshops.   I. Title.
  LB1576.C57758 2012
  372.62´3–dc23

                                                                    2011040924

10 9 8 7 6 5 4 3 2

Sr. Sponsoring Editor: Lauren Davis
Production Editor: Lauren Davis
Copyeditor: Andrew Miller
Designer and Compositor: Publishing Synthesis, Ltd.
Cover Designer: Dave Strauss, 3FoldDesign

Also Available from Eye On Education

Empowering Students to Write and Re-Write:
Standards-Based Strategies for Middle and High School Teachers
Warren E. Combs

Awakening Brilliance in the Writer's Workshop:
Using Notebooks, Mentor Texts, and the Writing Process
Lisa Morris

Write With Me:
Partnering With Parents in Writing Instruction
Lynda Wade Sentz

Successful Student Writing Through Formative Assessment
Harry Grover Tuttle

Teaching Grammar: What Really Works
Amy Benjamin and Joan Berger

Vocabulary at the Center
Amy Benjamin and John T. Crow

Motivating Every Student in Literacy
(Including the Highly Unmotivated!)
Sandra K. Athans and Denise Ashe Devine

Literacy From A to Z:
Engaging Students in Reading, Writing, Speaking and Listening
Barbara R. Blackburn

Building a Culture of Literacy Month-by-Month
Hilarie Davis

Literacy Leadership Teams
Pamela S. Craig

Active Literacy Across the Curriculum
Heidi Hayes Jacobs

Meet the Author

Warren E. Combs, Ph.D., is founder of Erincort Consulting, Inc., of Athens, Georgia, a professional development firm committed to the use of peak-performance strategies in the teaching of writing. A longtime researcher in the teaching of writing, he promotes classroom action research as the model for rigorous teaching and learning. He is a speaker, trainer and author of more than nineteen titles in the teaching of writing, writing to learn content standards, and sentence-combining practice. There have been significant increases in student performance on tests of ELA, math, science, social studies and writing in classroom action research at schools that undergo his training. He coauthored *The Writing Process* and authored *Empowering Students to Write and Re-Write* in addition to several journal articles and white papers. Topics on which he regularly speaks include Writing to Learn the Math Curriculum (CTAE, ELA, Science, Social Studies), Writer's Workshop for the Common Core, Classroom Action Research Made Easy and Monitoring the Progress of Young Writers.

Dr. Combs has worked with administrators, teachers, and directly with students in a host of K–12 schools across the Southeast and Midwest. His signature is demonstrating key practices in the teaching of writing with students while teachers observe from the perimeter of the room. He holds a B.A. in English, an M.A. in English linguistics and a Ph.D. in child development and English education.

Acknowledgements

In creating the Writing Cycle, I recognize my debt to dozens of K–12 teachers from Alabama, Georgia, North Carolina, South Carolina, South Dakota and Tennessee for their patience in trying out the Writing Cycle in all of its various versions.

Free Downloads

This book is accompanied by Free Downloads, which are available on Eye On Education's Web site as Adobe Acrobat files. The downloads include handouts for students and teachers, as well as session guides for professional development. Permission has been granted to purchasers of this book to download these resources and print them.

You can access these downloads by visiting Eye On Education's Web site: www.eyeoneducation.com. Click FREE DOWNLOADS or search or browse our Web site to find this book, and then scroll down for downloading instructions.

You'll need your book buyer access code: WWC-7192-8

Index of Downloads

Handouts for Students and Teachers

Sentence Chart (page 131)

Scoring Rubric (page 50)

Writing Cycle Log for Teacher Expectations (page 21)

Writing Cycle Log for Student Self-Check (page 22)

Study Guides for Professional Development Teams

Session 1 Guide (use after Chapters 1–5)

Session 2 Guide (use after Chapters 6–11)

Session 3 Guide (use after Chapters 12–13)

Session 4 Guide (use after Chapters 14–15)

Foreword

There is enough data to show that a large percentage of our students are arriving at colleges lacking the basic writing skills required for higher education or the workplace. The reports from the National Commission on Writing (2003, 2004 and 2005) have brought this dire situation to the consciousness of the American public.

Improving students' writing abilities requires improving teachers' proficiency and competency with our written language. During the last two decades there has been a great deal of attention paid to this aspect of literacy, through continuing education courses and in-service professional development. Many colleges have strengthened their teacher education programs to include a greater focus on writing. However, the move to educate in-service teachers about guiding students to competently articulate their thoughts on paper still remains a daunting task.

There are a few reasons that this task is so difficult:

- If we survey the language continuum—from listening to writing—it is evident that becoming a skilled writer is the most complex part of our language to learn and teach others.
- Few teachers indicate that they had a K–12 or college instructor who taught them how to write and how to teach their students to do the same.
- Many of those who have mastered this craft and provide guidance through face-to-face professional learning sessions are able to provide training at the "awareness" level, mostly through one- or two-day workshop sessions. The likelihood of these sessions to actually change practice is miniscule.
- Many schools do not understand the value of on-site coaching support in assisting teachers with the transfer of complex skills, learned in a workshop, into classroom practice. This type of follow-up support is thus seldom envisioned.
- Even when the vision for classroom coaching support exists, implementing it effectively is often cost prohibitive.

The best practices embedded in the writer's workshop approach have been touted by many as ideals appropriate for stemming the tide of basic illiteracy in this area. I am a believer in this approach. However, as an administrator, I struggled with providing effective training and support for teachers in my school districts to implement these practices. Whereas the instructional framework in the workshop model was easy to conceptualize (whether it was being explained by Nancie Atwell, a Four Blocks consultant, or some other expert), implementing the day-to-day key instructional practices of the model was overwhelming and difficult.

My search for ways to support teachers implement the practices of writer's workshop led me to a framework called the Writing Cycle. As I examined it closely, I realized that it contained the structure my teachers needed to execute writer's workshop with fidelity. I playfully call it "writer's workshop with training wheels." After experiencing writer's workshop training in several different settings, I felt that I had found a model that embraced all the research-based practices of writing but also had the appropriate amount of structure to guide teachers, whether they were novices or experts at writing. With this approach, they could stay the course and guide students successfully though the process of learning to write in a particular genre. I was ecstatic!

I have been a professional development consultant for the last twenty-five years. I have been involved in training in-service teachers here in the United States, and in Canada, Bermuda and Jamaica. I have also attended literacy workshops with experts from all over this country, and from the outset I could clearly see that using the Writing Cycle as a foundation for supporting writer's workshop would keep teachers and students from getting lost in the wilderness of this instructional framework. The Writing Cycle could be their guide through this forest.

So I was excited to learn that Dr. Warren Combs, creator of the Writing Cycle, was authoring a book that detailed his easy approach to guiding teachers to the Common Core State Standards for the teaching of writing. *Writer's Workshop for the Common Core* is such an appropriate title for describing the contents and the facility teachers could experience in meeting core standards without diluting the workshop model.

I have worked closely with Dr. Combs in my school district for the last three years. He has trained both elementary and secondary teachers in the use of this Writing Cycle. Furthermore, he has provided on-site support through classroom demonstrations and coaching visits. Teachers who have implemented the Writing Cycle with fidelity have not only been pleased by the ease with which they have been able to implement some key practices in writer's workshop, but in the growth of their students' writing abilities and their confidence in viewing themselves as writers. This school year, those elementary schools that implemented the Writing Cycle through Dr. Combs's Working Portfolio were pleased with the 7- to 21-point gains on the fifth-grade state writing assessment.

Teachers are pleased with the practical tools to support writer's workshop embedded in the process of using the Writing Cycle, including the entire writing process, students' self-assessments, specific strategies for revision and proofreading that build on students' strength, the use of rubrics, guided peer assessment, a scoring system that easily translates into letter grades and an independent assessment at the end of each cycle.

Dr. Combs's training as a linguist, background as a university professor and his broad experience as a practitioner, educational consultant, coach and master teacher is reflected in *Writer's Workshop for the Common Core*. This work reflects wisdom gained from years of experience involved in working closely with in-service teachers and their students.

If you are already using writer's workshop effectively, then the strategies in this book will only help you to sharpen your saw. If you have a desire to begin the implementation of this workshop approach, then this book will surely assist you with planning and making your opening moves. Do not stop reading until you clearly understand the steps involved in carrying out a Writing Cycle, and you will see how it can guide you to implement writer's workshop with dispatch. In addition to providing this valuable information, this book will also make you aware of accompanying materials that will help you to manage the "paper" involved with this approach and enable your students to become more independent learners.

Hats off to you, Dr. Combs. A book that makes writer's workshop with the Common Core Standards manageable and doable is a book that is long overdue.

Ingrid Jones, Ph.D.
Professional Learning Specialist
Catoosa County Schools
Ringgold, Georgia

Contents

Introduction

The Design of the Common Core Standards

By emphasizing required achievements, the Standards leave room for teachers, curriculum developers and states to determine how those goals should be reached and what additional topics should be addressed. Thus, the Standards do not mandate such things as a particular writing process or the full range of meta-cognitive strategies that students may need to monitor and direct their thinking and learning. Teachers are thus free to provide students with whatever tools and knowledge their professional judgment and experiences identify as most helpful for meeting the goals set out in the standards.

"Writing gives me such enormous pleasure, and I'm a much happier (and therefore nicer) person when I'm doing it."

—Julie Myerson, author and critic

Writer's Workshop for the Common Core presents the journey that I have taken with teachers, curriculum directors, district administrators and state department leaders throughout my career. In our patient work together, we tried various instructional tools and strategies, abandoned many and embraced only those that worked the most often with the most students. Interestingly, some of the most critical suggestions came from students themselves, suggestions repeated again and again until we understood the significance of what the students were saying.

You see, I am a trained student of English linguists who enjoyed appointments in an English department, linguistics program and college of education at the Universities of Minnesota and Georgia. There I taught a mix of graduate-level courses to liberal arts students and teachers of general and special education students. I relished teaching History of the English Language and Language Acquisition of Children for which I was well prepared. At first it was a stretch to teach Language Studies for Teachers of English and Normal Language Development for special education teachers. Yet these were the courses that were more important to the in-service teachers I met each semester. They saw that the acquisition of speech presented a clear road map for the teaching of writing with a focus on *know-how* knowledge of writing before *know-about* knowledge. Yet when they returned to their schools, they found few tools in place to let their students learn how to write before they taught them about the way language worked.

I first met writer's workshop when I shared a spot with other first-time presenters, Nancie Atwell and her colleagues, at the National Council of Teachers of English (NCTE). Atwell's group had it right: focus on learning how to write before learning about writing. I left the session thinking, All is right with the world of the teaching of writing.

In the years since, however, I heard numerous teachers opine, We use the workshop model to a T, but our students' test scores don't budge!

The response: Keep teaching writer's workshop. Teaching writing is not about numbers or the standards. It's about freeing students to create. Then the month before a writing test, teach students about the test. Tests are a necessary evil.

My jaw dropped. That advice doesn't jibe with what we know about how the human brain learns.

Not every proponent of writer's workshop has this take. In *The Energy to Teach*, Donald Graves takes an entire chapter to admonish us teachers of writing to "Take Energy from Assessment." He points to an important and close connection between the teaching of writing and the assessment of writing that produces a number value that educators, parents and students understand. Graves asserts that assessment can be a positive source of energy for us in designing key practices in the teaching of writing. *Writer's Workshop for the Common Core* invites you to tune in to that vision of how to join the data of your students' performance (summative assessment) with key classroom practices (formative assessment) in the teaching of writing. With the tools and strategies presented in this book, my teacher colleagues and I are seeing this connection with increasing clarity.

Actually, using writer's workshop outside of the context of the Common Core State Standards compounds the workload for teachers. Grave's notes this in his foreword to Nancie Atwell's *In the Middle*: "Beyond such incredible student writing works a pragmatic, literate professional. The key word is *works*. Nancie works her tail off. The faint-hearted need not apply for this kind of teaching." No wonder that message of the remarkable power of writer's workshop has not filtered down to the rank-and-file teachers of writing. What is attractive about an approach to teaching writing that may not impact student performance but is certain to wear you out?

Writer's Workshop for the Common Core alters this view of writer's workshop. It forwards an undeniable truth about human learning. Authentic learning of any subject increases performance on tests of knowledge in that subject. And the increased performance of students does not have to come at great expense to the teacher. Chapters 1 through 3 describe the evolution of the Writing Cycle—an instructional tool that solders the connection between learning (writer's workshop) and testing (state writing tests). As I point out in chapter 4, the words we teachers use in talking with students about writing have to change before peak-performance writing translates into peak-performance testing of written expression. Chapter 5 wraps up the introduction with a look at a classroom of peak-performance writers and the data from tests of written expression from students like them. In these schools and more, students of the Writing Cycle are working as hard as their teachers, and none of them would call their work *hard*.

To be sure, the teaching of writing is arguably the most complicated undertaking in the K–12 curriculum. That doesn't mean, however, that it has to be hard work. Getting students to write has always carried an unexplained attraction for me. Almost every day that students write with me across seven states, I discover new angles for triggering students' writing instincts. The quest is satisfying in itself.

In the shadow of the Common Core State Standards, the next chapters map out instructional tools and strategies that ease the stress of teaching writing. They emphasize formative assessment of the writing process one step at a time in a Working Portfolio (a twenty-four-page booklet) of the Writing Cycle. Chapters 6 through 11 focus on first drafts in a weekly pacing guide that accommodates both faster and slower learners:

- Analyzing or creating standards-based writing topic prompts (chapter 6)
- Prewriting (chapter 7)
- Drafting for special needs and gifted students (chapter 8)
- Three volleys at revision (chapters 9 through 11)

The following chapters focus on what students can learn to love to do with final drafts: proofreading (chapter 12) and scoring (chapter 13), two skills teachers often shy away from. Then we turn to summative assessment and celebration. Chapter 14 presents an Unassisted Writing Sample that amounts to a mock writing test of the genre taught in the previous Working Portfolio. Chapter 15 reminds us of the power of publication: only authentic celebration of writing on the terms of the student writers will do. The epilogue charts a path that any pair of teachers can follow in their first experience with a Writing Cycle.

Throughout *Writer's Workshop for the Common Core*, two strands support ready implementation of the ideas presented. The first includes references to the instructional tools in the book available as free downloadable pages at www.eyeoneducation.com and www.writingtowin.com. Go ahead and download the Student Exemplar of a Working Portfolio so you have the big picture in mind as you work through the detailed strategies. (Page numbers for additional instructional tools and strategies refer to a companion volume, *A Writing Cycle for Writer's Workshop*, available at www.writingtowin.com.) The second strand, a guide for professional learning teams (PLT) appears on the Eye On Education Web site in a sequence of four PLT sessions. Directions for setting up teams of teachers to study this book together are found in that guide. We provide the sequence for learning; you choose the timeline for implementing it.

Writer's Workshop for the Common Core addresses teachers and students simultaneously. Comments to teachers appear in standard font, and the model scripts to students are set off. The instructional tools and strategies work for me in classes of gifted students as well as with those who have special needs. Writing is the ultimate differentiator; it automatically adjusts to all learning styles and ability levels of students. Happily, you get to find that out for yourself. So at first, use the provided scripts with my regards; they are the product of years of testing and adjusting precise wording of concrete tasks that led to authentic writing. The first Writing Cycle helped my children—Cortney, Erin and Taylor—write with authenticity at home as they wrote along with me. The improved Writing Cycle in these pages is working for their children—Bella, Avery and Timothy—as they delight in writing with Pop Pop. Join us by inviting your students to write with you.

Here's to authentic writing!

Warren E. Combs
November 2011

Chapter 1

The Need for Writer's Workshop to Work with Ease

> **Common Core State Standards for ELA and Literacy**
>
> As a natural outgrowth of meeting the charge to define college and career readiness, the standards also lay out a vision of what it means to be a literate person in the twenty-first century . . . In short, students who meet the Standards develop the skills in reading, writing, speaking and listening that are the foundation for any creative and purposeful expression in language.

"For the first time in twenty years, teaching the writing process is enjoyable; actually, it's easy."

—Melody Moore, grade 5 teacher

I admit it: I absolutely delight in using writer's workshop. It fits me and my teaching style hand in glove. I cannot imagine a better way to reach the vision of the Common Core State Standards for writing. The first time I saw it presented, I knew it could make peak-performing writers out of most students. So why am I writing this book? And why should you read it? I'm writing it because in working with teachers across the United States, the majority of teachers of writing remain untouched by writer's workshop. In addition, I have witnessed the evolution of a framework that I call the Writing Cycle. When teachers use the Writing Cycle with fidelity, they experience increased ease in implementing writer's workshop. When students experience the Writing Cycle, they increase their performance as strong, independent writers. Impact data shows that the strategies embedded in the Writing Cycle have helped to produce better results in implementing all of the following:

- The steps in the writing process
- The six traits of writing
- Key practices of learning in the classroom

Additionally, the Writing Cycle helps improve scores on benchmark tests of written expression better than I could have imagined.

In many schools I visit, teachers beg for a step-by-step guide, a book that directs them in the use of the strategies in this enhancement tool that I call the Writing Cycle. See if you fall into one of these groups.

- The first group is trained extensively in writer's workshop. These teachers embrace it and have developed their unique version of the model, but they see little positive, and sometimes even negative, impact on students' scores on tests of written expression. They work hard and feel that their students grow as writers, but that growth doesn't register when students take writing tests.
- Teachers in the second group use the language of writer's workshop—mini-lesson, author's chair, conferencing, writing portfolios, rituals and routines. Yet they keep the routines they have always used intact. They report little evidence of the independent writers that they and their administrators expected.
- The third group met writer's workshop and rejected it in the process of trying it out. The benefits of the model did not convince them to put the work required into it. Currently, this is a much larger group than I had thought possible.
- The fourth group equally intrigues me. It includes teachers who have yet to meet writer's workshop. Again, in 2011, this is a larger group than I ever expected.

So whether you employ writer's workshop in your classroom, reject it or haven't heard of it yet, you and your students could benefit from a test drive with the Writing Cycle. But before we move into the showroom of Writing Cycles, I need to make sure we all are thinking about writer's workshop in the same way.

Writer's Workshop

The first time I met writer's workshop, I was hooked; it was the first viable model for the teaching of writing that I had come across, and I haven't changed my mind about that. Earlier approaches to the teaching of writing taught students about writing before they allowed them to get down to writing; writer's workshop empowers students to write from the beginning.

Advocates of writer's workshop have worked diligently; the model has emerged and resurged over the years, reigniting interest from one generation of teachers to the next. It is the single model presented by major publishing houses of professional development in the teaching of writing. The model is intuitively sound and promoted by the widespread and vibrant National Writing Project (NWP). NWP summer institutes energized many graduates, who completely reformed their approach to the teaching of writing. The workshop model has spread to other strands of the curriculum as the hallmark of good teaching. The call for proposals in the Race to the Top requires a workshop model. As long as we offer workshop-based learning experience guided by brain research, we are on solid ground. Figure 1.1 below summarizes typical elements of writer's workshop.

Figure 1.1   The Writer's Workshop Model

Mini-lesson—**ML** (7–10 min); work time—**W** (15–20 min); close—**C** (7–10 min)

Day →		Monday	Tuesday	Wednesday	Thursday	Friday
Working Portfolio	M L	**Mini-lessons** begin with establishing the rituals and routines of writer's workshop. Teachers have standard routines in mind but lead students in arriving at ones that meet or exceed their expectations. • Include craft or skills lesson selected by teachers based on their observations of student writing • Include models of writing from professional writing, classroom teachers and former students • Target whole-group or small-group lessons				
	W	**Work sessions** • Provide time and support for students to practice the rituals and routines of the mini-lesson • Include learning centers and workstations with reference tools for various steps of the writing process • Include posted exemplars of student work on current writing standards for students to consult • Target largely individual work				
	C	**Author's chair close** helps students share their written efforts with a partner, small group or whole group to receive coaching from peers trained in constructive responses. • Mention of what engages them, what they want to know more about and questions about the writing				

Writer's workshop can be powerful in its simplicity. It

- Admonishes teachers to keep fine-tuning writing lessons so that they become more and more concise and easier for students to follow—thus, the term *mini-lesson.*
- Protects the majority of class time as a work session in which students work out their understanding of the mini-lesson as teachers facilitate their progress.
- Concludes with a closure activity; students move into preassigned small groups to share their progress in the work session for constructive response.

That's it. This idea that teachers lead each new group of students in creating rituals and routines that meet stated standards is simple, yet undeniably ambitious. Fortunately, versions of mini-lessons, portfolios, ideas for conferencing and employing author's chairs abound. There is a version of writer's workshop out there to fit every teacher in the profession. The NWP Web site alone includes more ideas for using writer's workshop than anyone could read in a lifetime, much less use. Professional development books and Web sites of hundreds of writing programs, publishing companies, schools and teachers add to the glut of resources.

A number of books guide the design of a classroom to nurture developing young writers, so that is not the purpose of this book. In Denise Leograndis's *Launching the Writing Workshop: A Step-by-Step Guide in Photographs,* her stated goals—1) to build a safe writing community; 2) to establish rituals and routines; 3) to generate lots of thinking, talk and writing; and 4) to develop the understanding that all good writing has meaning, detail, structure and pacing—are achieved in "The Four-Week Launch" (Leograndis, p. 10). You can't get much more specific and intentional than she. The pictures of her classroom arrangement throughout provide graphic clarity for Leograndis's written description. In chapter 4, I recommend replacing her terms, *meaning, structure* and *details,* with more student-friendly terms. Otherwise, she represents writer's workshop as clearly as is possible.

The Difficulty of Teaching Writing

The difficulty of teaching writing remains hidden in the simplicity of the writer's workshop model, and the model often leaves well-intentioned, dedicated teachers frustrated and weary from trying to make writer's workshop a reality in their classrooms. In spite of all of the viable resources available from an Internet search of "writer's workshop," teachers are as likely to feel overwhelmed by the resources as helped.

It was difficult for me to admit this. With eyes wide open to learn, I saw many teachers overpowered by the very instructional tools created to make their lives easy. Oh, they were excited when they met writer's workshop and used the activities provided in the training when they returned to their classes. Yet they faltered at keeping the model moving from there. These teachers voiced a full range of observations and questions, and I listened to their voices, treating each with respect and concern. Once I let myself look for ways to help teachers instead of defending a model that worked beautifully for me, the Writing Cycle emerged as a key tool in dealing with the complexities of teaching writing. Like a set of training wheels for writer's workshop, the Writing Cycle makes it possible—and even easy—for teachers to hand over the strategies of all writing tasks to students while helping them become confident, independent writers. After all, this is the stated goal of writer's workshop. It is just unfortunate that it has not happened for more teachers in every aspect of the teaching of writing.

The First Set of Teachers' Voices

The voices I heard most often said, "You don't know my students. They can't deal with all this freedom of choice in writer's workshop. They haven't a clue about where to begin writing. You really aren't telling me to just let them find their way, are you?"

Actually, I wasn't. Obviously, these teachers received a different message in writer's workshop than I. Yet when I said that they misunderstand the model, it heightened instead of relieved their anxiety.

For this group of teachers, the first practice of the Writing Cycle that helps writer's workshop work with ease emerged: quantify teacher expectations. In his book *Social Theory and Social Structure*, Robert Merton cites the undeniable impact of the self-fulfilling prophecy. Whether we state our expectations for students or not, they somehow figure them out and unconsciously go about fulfilling them. So this is the message to the twenty-first-century teachers of writing: set specific, quantified expectations of writing that demonstrate your belief to your students that they can meet a stated standard of writing. Quantify the number of sentences, paragraphs or pages as well as expectations of audience, purpose and tone.

Admittedly, I have colleagues who feel that adding a framework to the writer's workshop increases the threat of formula writing. Yet just the opposite is true. A recent graduate of a two-day intensive training session testified, "All this quantifying of expectations just seemed too structured for me at first, but the writing of us teachers these two days is surprisingly authentic, and I can see authentic writing emerging in the writing of my students." And indeed she did—and still does.

So with every writing task, quantify your expectations for all students so they are free to focus on what they are thinking. Curiously, as these voices seemed satisfied by my response, I heard additional voices of teachers that led to further, simple enhancements to writer's workshop. The key practices of the Writing Cycle fell into place like cherries in a row of a winning pull on a Las Vegas slot machine.

<table>
<tr><td>Teachers' Voices</td><td>"The student exemplars of writing in many books on writer's workshop come from students eager to share their experiences. Many of my students don't see their personal experiences as ones to share. Also, they do not visualize readers who are interested in their ideas."</td></tr>
</table>

A simple solution? Prompt students to write about experiences that they have in school. With the Common Core State Standards, our classrooms are becoming a near-perfect universe of students with shared learning experiences. So in the Writing Cycle, teachers find an archive of writing topic prompts that prepare students to exceed standards of state or national writing assessment (see chapters 3, 6 and 7). Then writing becomes nonfiction writing assessments based on what students meet in their health, fine arts, foreign language, math, science, social studies or technology curriculum.

<table>
<tr><td>Teachers' Voices</td><td>"We teach solid mini-lessons and read models of writing for students to follow. We have 60 minutes for writing each day, and our students make little use of the time. We're wearing ourselves out moving about the classroom keeping the students motivated and on task."</td></tr>
</table>

It's unrealistic to expect students to stay engaged in thoughtful writing for 60 minutes; 30 to 40 is maximal (see chapter 2). Practice writing what you have prompted your students to write; start writing first and invite them to write along. Then time each writing task with limits that drive home a sense of urgency. You'll be amazed at the transformation of student writers in your class. Don't protect your students from the struggle and the stretch to write out their thoughts. In your peripheral vision, watch out for any outlier who needs a boost.

"We're good teachers; parents ask for their students to be placed in our classes, but we're at our wits end. Yet we are told to differentiate instruction for every student writing on different topics at different steps of the writing process. Does anyone believe that this is a real-world possibility with beginning writers?"

Beginning writers need the scaffolding of key practices in small or whole groups. With its instructional guides, checklists, rubrics, organizers and strategies, the Writing Cycle provides students with foundation practices in authentic writing.

"We've shown videotapes of mini-lessons that we just love. We've read our own writing as models. We identify model writing in professional writing. We teach the language of the writing genre, yet our students write little and see little need to write more. The culture for writing is just not emerging in our classrooms like our workshop trainer demonstrated for us. What's wrong?"

In the Writing Cycle, teacher expectations are quantified, and students self-assess the degree to which they meet your expectations. You can quantify and students can count. When you tell students that their self-assessment goes directly into your grade book (unless you find a good reason for changing it), they will meet and exceed expectations. Require and help students to self-assess each writing task in the writing process.

"We're convinced of the power of peer coaching, so we involve students in every step of the writing process. Every time a student coaches, we have to go behind them to see if they have given good advice. This seems like needless extra work, especially when some peers' suggestion derail the writing."

It is needless extra work: learn the best times and use only concrete, specific strategies for peer coaching (see chapter 4 and the PALS appendix). The Writing Cycle recommends only these specific, intentional peer responses. After students prewrite, draft or revise, peers use

- Author's chair routines to identify the degree to which writers met the teacher's quantified expectations
- Peer-Assisted Learning System (PALS) strategies to identify specific features of writing

Since conferencing causes pain, take your eyes off it. Focus on whole-group and small-group instruction. Most students have similar problems in writing and can be conferenced in groups. Work one-on-one only with students who present unique issues.

So what is this Writing Cycle that answers the concerns of all of these voices of teachers? How can it help you do a better job implementing writer's workshop? Chapter 3 provides the answers, but a little more background is necessary to help you understand and appreciate the sound and deliberate metamorphosis of the Writing Cycle.

It all started with The Pyramid of Average Learning Retention Rates that I met early in my career (See Figure 1.2 on page 9.) The data clearly show that listening and reading have the lowest retention rates of any classroom modes of learning. When we ask students to listen or read, we cannot be certain of the degree to which they are doing either with comprehension. The encoding skills of writing and speaking significantly boost retention because they both require observable practice by doing. You can see or hear the degree to which students reconfigured what you taught in their own words.

Since there's not enough time in a day to hear your students explain what they know orally, writing is the language art that boosts learning retention most efficiently. Yet almost all of the U.S. federal dollars that support literacy go to reading. It is no wonder that most classroom teachers argue that students must learn to read before they can write. Interestingly, this nod to reading overlooks the vast majority of U. S. kindergartners who show up hesitant as readers and boldly confident as writers—drawing, scribbling or indeed crafting words, phrases and sentences with intent and meaning. When teachers let their students write before they read, their growth as writers leads their growth as readers . . . and then their growth as readers leads their writing. It's a phenomenal model of symbiosis at work.

I will not attempt to diffuse the debate over whether reading or writing is acquired first. It misses the point. The data are clear: the average learning retention rate for reading over time is 10%. Educational leaders and politicians couldn't overcome the limits of the human brain with tsunamis of dollars. The 75% retention rate resides on the opposite side of the literacy coin in writing; we need to call a halt to the discussion of which comes first and let writing do its magic.

Figure 1.2 The Pyramid of Average Learning Retention Rates

Why we write to learn

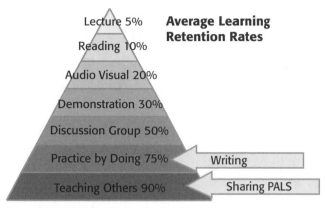

Source: National Training Laboratories, Bethel, Maine

There's a long and distinguished tradition of careful study showing that writing precedes or grows in tandem with reading in young writers. Jean Piaget (*The Language and Thought of the Child,* 1926), Noam Chomksy (*Aspects of the Theory of Syntax,* 1969) and psycholinguists Frank Smith (*Understanding Reading,* 1971) and Courtney Cazden (*Child Language and Education,* 1972) all presented these studies better than I. The Language Experience model for teaching reading and writing in kindergarten is still the most productive writing-reading strategy for beginning language learners. So let's continue the quest to help the teacher voices crying out for the teaching of writing to work with ease. Come along with me; enjoy seeing how eight respected practices from inside and outside of the teaching of writing came together in the Writing Cycle. It was certainly a welcomed sight for me to behold.

Looking Back

In your response journal, describe two benefits that you see in your understanding of the writer's workshop model for you as a teacher in your present classes.

Looking Ahead

What is coming up in your curriculum that will benefit from some adjustments in key elements of writer's workshop?

Chapter 2

The Common Core and Research Behind the Writing Cycle

Common Core State Standards for ELA and Literacy

The Standards set requirements not only for English language arts (ELA) but also for literacy in history/social studies, science and technical subjects. Just as students must learn to read, write, speak, listen and use language effectively in a variety of content areas, so too must the Standards specify the literacy skills and understandings required for college and career readiness in multiple disciplines. Literacy standards ... [count on teachers] using their content area expertise to help students meet the particular challenges of reading, writing, speaking, listening and language in their respective field.

"Consistent nonfiction writing assessments in every subject [boosts achievement] in math, science and social studies [and] is also effective in improving performance on writing tests and extended response items."
—Douglas Reeves, *The Learning Leader*

A remarkable turn of events in my home state cast the effect of writer's workshop on scores of written expression in a completely different light. In 1996, the state offered writer's workshop to over 340 elementary and middle schools that were defined as failing. What an opportunity for 10,000 teachers and almost 200,000 students! Unfortunately, the results on independent assessments of writing in grades 5 and 8 were all over the charts. A few schools posted sterling and significant improvements on tests of written expression; more posted decreases in student performance, and over half posted no significant difference at all.

As I tried to understand this sobering performance of a model that I experience as sound, I was haunted by one question: why don't more of the implementations of writer's workshop deliver the results that I know they can? No doubt, there were various explanations for why writer's workshop failed in so many schools. I knew one thing: I couldn't turn a blind eye to the fact that many teachers who tried writer's workshop did not experience satisfactory results. I wasn't willing to blame it on the teachers, the students, the administrators, the timing or the way it was implemented. If anything could be done to the model itself to make it reach more teachers and students with success, I was for it.

I turned to the work of respected teachers, researchers and authors for ideas that make the teaching of writing work with ease. In the teaching of writing, Donald Murray, Steve Graham, Robert Marzano, Flannery O'Connor and Peter Elbow caught my attention. From the wider community of teaching and learning, Douglas Reeves, Tom Merton, Rick Stiggins and David Sousa addressed the issues surrounding writer's workshop. Together, those leaders pointed to eight conclusions that apply to the teaching of writing that I began putting into practice as students wrote with me. The combined impact of these ideas was gratifying—once I successfully employed them simultaneously.

Picture these practices as eight spinning plates on poles in a circus act. The performer doesn't start all the plates at once. She moves on from the first plate only once it is balanced and spinning with rhythmic speed. When all the plates are spinning perfectly, the audience applauds; when all eight practices of an effective writing routine work well, students, administrators and parents join the teacher in applause.

Fortunately this is where the comparison to spinning plates ends. When the performer sees the first tell-tale wobble, she brings her act to a close. Thankfully, these practices in teaching writing aren't plates. Students internalize them with ease, and when all eight practices work together for them, they want to repeat them—as they do all new and rewarding experiences in their growing worlds. Once they

- Watch you write and hear you read your model of the writing that you assigned, they look to you for a repeat performance.
- Experience the benefit from writing about new knowledge in their fine arts, foreign language, health, literature, math, science, social studies or technology curriculum, they want the benefit to continue.
- Self-assess their performance and see that their assessment affects the grades on their report card, they insist on staying in charge of their own performance.
- Focus on word study and sentence study tasks within the context of the writing process, they see them as refreshing alternatives to the rigors of writer's workshop.

In short, your students' brains view the Writing Cycle as productive and seek to return to it again and again, at first at your prompting, but in later years, in the writing required of adults in a first-world culture.

To be sure, the minute I put the benefit for students ahead of precedence or convenience for teachers, changes that enhanced writer's workshop became obvious. Most of them came from research outside of the teaching of writing; two were just plain common sense. Let's start with six research-based conclusions.

Research-based practice #1: Rein in the range of topic choices for students to choices within the Common Core State Standards for writing.

From the research of the Leadership and Learning Center, Douglas Reeves highlights the power of consistent "nonfiction writing assessment" in every subject of the curriculum. All topics are within the realm of students' experiences because they experience them in the classroom. Writing serves as a vehicle for learning both content standards and standards of written expression. All writing topic prompts of the Writing Cycle empower students to fashion a personal understanding of the Common Core State Standards. In short, writing about the curriculum levels the playing field for all students regardless of the level of literacy their home life provides. Research-based conclusion #1 seconds the call of the Common Core State Standards for special emphasis on informational/explanatory texts.

Research-based practice #2: In each mini-lesson, set time limits for the resulting student work session that compels students to write without hesitation. Effective time limits signal to the student brain, "I had better get to work."

David Sousa's brain studies describe Primetimes I, II and III for learning in the brain. Primetime I is the first 7 to 10 minutes of a learning experience, the time at which the brain seeks parameters for learning, a neat window of time for a mini-lesson in writer's workshop. Primetime II is the last 7 to 10 minutes of a learning experience, the time window the brain needs to pull it all together, clear support for author's chair: well-defined routines for student sharing and peer response. Primetime III is the middle 15 to 20 minutes for a student work session. A 35- to 40-minute writing lesson conforms to how the brain learns; longer time periods for writing deliver diminishing returns.

Research-based practice #3: Quantify expectations for each student work session. Then empower students to use a corresponding simple rubric for the self-assessment of every writing task.

From the research of the Assessment Training Institute, Rick Stiggins promotes the power of frequent student self-assessment (formative assessment) in every course of the curriculum. Whenever students assess their own progress in a course of study, they score 30% to 80% higher on tests of knowledge of the content. In order for students to self-assess each learning task with accuracy and consistency, teachers must quantify their expectations. Self-assessment includes responding to questions, identifying features of writing and interacting with peers using concrete, specific strategies. The role of teachers? Review student self-assessments and adjust them to align with stated expectations.

Research-based practice #4: Call on, develop and archive concrete, specific writing strategies for each step of the writing process in the Common Core State Standards. Present them as requirements until students demonstrate mastery of each. Then retain them as options available to students throughout the writing process.

Steve Graham and Dolores Perin's report to the Carnegie Corporation of New York, *Writing Next* (2007), examined studies of specific, concrete writing strategies and set product goals. Eighteen studies demonstrated the significant impact of specific, concrete planning and revision strategies on writing achievement when compared with instruction without assigned strategies. These results held true for full-range classes as well as learning disabled and low-achieving classes. Five studies presented treatments that set specific product goals. Students prompted to include specific, common persuasive elements outperformed students who simply followed a persuasive model. Five studies established the efficacy of concrete prewriting strategies versus quick writes or freestyle webbing.

Research-based practice #5: Prompt students to write multiple first drafts in a stated mode or genre. Then require students to take only one of them through the writing process, giving them credit for meeting standards of revision, editing, final evaluation and presentation.

From Donald Murray's research and experience comes a marked conclusion: it is more effective for student writers to work through the writing process fewer times more thoroughly than to take every piece of writing through the entire writing process. In every Writing Cycle, then, students write three first drafts based on three separate topic prompts; they then select the one they like the best to revise, proofread, score and publish.

> **Research-based practice #6:** Schedule breaks in the arduous process of writing to focus on word study and sentence study to support the skills needed in the context of the writing.

Vocabulary and sentence structure have always played a large part of instruction in writing. Yet either the research of Robert Marzano or Steve Graham shows that there are some word and sentence studies that complement the writing process and some that detract from it. Marzano has shown that word study can be enjoyable *and* related to national standards presented in word groups formed by meaning instead of structure (spelling, phonics). Graham notes that sentence study that requires students to put sentences together impacts students' scores of written expression positively. Sentence study that requires students to take sentences apart or correct them is more likely to have a negative impact. In the Writing Cycle, students meet word or sentence study at least twice a week, providing a healthy break from focus on writing in a way that continues to effect growth in writing.

There are two commonsense practices.

> **Commonsense practice #1:** Set a pace at which all students focus on one step of the writing process at a time. Plan learning activities within that window of time that permit students to work at different paces.

Classrooms hum with eager learners who work together through learning sequences together. In math, we ask students to study fractions or problem-solving strategies at the same time; in physical education, students attend to physical tasks one at a time, together. But then, for some reason, in the teaching of writing, we let students take their own time in finding a topic and in working through each step of the writing process at will. Twenty-five students in widely different places along the writing process just does not work in most classrooms I have observed. One teacher's comment comes to mind: "Letting each student choose his/her own pace is like herding cats—not a lot of progress in that venture." I listen to comments like this from teachers who have abandoned practices that their students sorely need to acquire. They are symptoms that something needs to be done. In a Writing Cycle, for example, all students work on prewriting strategies at the same time. Yet within the time window scheduled for prewriting, students operate at their own pace, shifting in and out of word and sentence studies at their own pace.

> **Commonsense practice #2:** Conference one-on-one with students only as it is absolutely required. Train students to coach one another, using peer-assisted learning strategies.

In the work of Steve Graham, Bruce Saddler and Douglas and Lynn Fuchs, the Peer-Assisted Learning System (PALS) appears as an effective way to differentiate instruction. PALS offers a commonsense alternative to setting and maintaining regularly scheduled student-teacher conferences. Finding time to plan effective conferences with each of your students every other week is daunting; otherwise, we'd see a lot more conferencing going on. Besides, if students are progressing nicely (and numbers of them are), why break their rhythm with a prescheduled conference. In too many conferences that I observe, students let their teachers' ideas move their papers forward. Ultimately, every workshop session in a Writing Cycle concludes with PALS following concrete routines of sharing and responding.

Chapter 3 shows you how these research-based and commonsense practices come together in the Writing Cycle framework. In every school I introduce it, teachers and students add their own imagination and energy to the instructional guides, word banks, rubrics and strategies. These ready-made tools in the Writing Cycle exist to connect students to their best thoughts and liberate them to express them in authentic ways. Return to chapter 3 often to see how the Writing Cycle neatly archives all of the strategies of subsequent chapters.

Looking Back

In your response journal, describe two benefits that you readily see in the research that come together to inform a new way of implementing writer's workshop. How important is research outside the teaching of writing to forming an effective approach to the teaching of writing?

Looking Ahead

What is coming up in your curriculum that will benefit from the research-based and commonsense practices presented in this chapter?

Chapter 3

A First Look at the Writing Cycle

Common Core State Standards for Writing

Range of Writing—10. Write routinely over extended time frames (time for research, reflection and revision) and shorter time frames (a single sitting or a day or two) for a range of tasks, purposes and audiences.

"At first I thought the Writing Cycle too structured, but it consistently produces authentic student writing."

—Debbie Paine, academic coach

Most simply, the Writing Cycle is an instructional closet for your use that is filled with tested instructional tools:

- Instructional logs
- Model scripts
- Advance organizers
- Idea generators
- Checklists
- Charts
- Rubrics
- Response forms
- Archive of writing topic prompts
- Revision and proofreading strategies

The tools support six key practices.

1. Invite your students to write with you, using yourself as a model. Start writing with engagement in your Working Portfolio for Teachers. Free yourself from hovering over and "helping" students as they write. Most of that monitoring distracts them from writing. For sure, stop writing for an instant conference if a student shows signs of

being overwhelmed. As you model intense engagement in your own writing, an increasing number of students will follow in your wake.

2. Choose writing topics within the bounds of the math, reading, science or social studies curriculum.

3. Quantify expectations of all writing tasks and present students with a simple rubric for self-assessment.

4. Keep all writing tasks within the time limits recommended by brain research.

5. Schedule students to experience the writing process together one step at a time; have word- and sentence-study centers available for students who finish tasks early.

6. Make sure that students write on similar topics, genres and modes to take full advantage of the power of the Peer-Assisted Learning System.

So the Writing Cycle serves as an instructional scaffold that supports your and your students' thoughts as you move toward the standards of each mode or genre of writing. It provides concrete, specific strategies that writer's workshop leaves up to teachers to develop. It translates the design of an effective learning event (David Sousa, *How the Brain Works*) into the context of a writing classroom. In short, it integrates the theoretical (brain-based studies), philosophical (writer's workshop) and practical (Writing Cycle action research) foundations for teaching writing (see Figure 3.1 on page 18).

A well-executed Writing Cycle fits neatly into a nine-week grading period: seven weeks for a Working Portfolio (chapters 6 to 13) and two weeks for an Unassisted Writing Sample (chapter 14). See www.writingtowin. com for student exemplars of each. (For further support, see Combs 2011, *A Writing Cycle for Writer's Workshops*.) Most importantly, prompt your students to follow the workshop model each day and focus on one step of the writing process each week.

A Working Portfolio (formative assessment)

Week 1 task: Prewriting and first draft on a first topic (chapters 6 to 8)

Week 2 task: Prewriting and first draft on a second topic (chapters 6 to 8)

Week 3 task: Prewriting and first draft on a third topic (chapters 6 to 8)

Week 4 task: Revising one of the above first drafts; final draft (chapters 9 to 11)

Figure 3.1 Integrating Three Research Strands in Every Writing Task

Element	Brain-Based Studies	Writer's Workshop	A Writing Cycle
Opening 7–10 min	**Primetime I:** the launch time of an effective learning experience when the brain searches for a paradigm for learning to embrace.	**Mini-lesson:** introduction that focuses on one teaching point for the duration of the workshop. Usually a whole group instruction. Models mostly come from professional writers.	**Invite** students to write with you following specific strategies and quantified expectations. **Model** of your writing or that of a former student.
Work Session 15–20 min	**Primetime III:** the self-directed time in an effective learning experience when the brain explores the uses and options of a paradigm.	**Workshop:** time for students to use the teaching point of the mini-lesson in their own writing.	**Write:** time for students to use specific strategies or instructional tools to reach or exceed your expectations.
Closing 7–10 min	**Primetime II:** the end time of an effective learning experience, when the brain solidifies understanding and solders new knowledge to existing knowledge.	**Author's Chair:** students present their writing task to a partner, small group or whole group for conditioned and constructive response.	**Look:** read writing aloud in PALS for scripted peer response. **Learn:** the whole group lists the elements and benefits of the writing task.

Week 5 task: Proofreading the final draft with a cooperative group (chapter 12)

Week 6 task: Evaluating the final draft with a rubric (chapter 13)

Week 7 task: Publishing the final draft for an audience (chapter 13)

An Unassisted Writing Sample (summative assessment)

Week 8 task: Responding to a topic prompt from prewriting for a first draft to proofreading a final draft (chapter 14)

Week 9 task: Scoring students' unassisted writing using a standards-based rubric and a reliable scoring procedure (chapter 14)

Two instructional logs—a Writing Cycle Log for Teacher Expectations (Figure 3.2, page 21) and a Writing Cycle Log for Student Self-Check (Figure 3.3, page 22)—provide venues for dialogue between you and your students in the Writing Cycle framework. They provide

- For you, a reminder to quantify expectations for each writing task of the writing process that remain in view for nine weeks.
- For your students, a systematic way to inform you of their performance and to participate in their own learning.
- For parents and administrators, documentation in black-and-white of how you and your students work together as they acquire the standards.

When you and your students keep these two logs current, benefits abound.

- Student-teacher conferences run more efficiently.
- Student-teacher interactions about writing are clear and to the point.
- Administrators and colleagues visit without interrupting instruction.
- Parents are fully informed on their children's progress.

Compare the two logs on pages 21 and 22 completed by grade 3 teacher Ms. Song and her student, Jake, and see how they support a productive dialogue. For 1st Draft #1 on page 21, she set her expectation of mode C (character sketch), quantity of three paragraphs and the topic, "A favorite character you have met in reading this year."

Jake and his classmates understood that in meeting the target (◎), they were claiming a B or 85 points out of 100. For an A, or all hundred points, they had to exceed the stated expectations. On page 22, Jake claimed that he met the target by inserting a ◎ in the self-check column for his teacher's review. She responded in the points column with a 90. Apparently, she felt that Jake's first draft actually exceeded the target enough to earn five additional points. No further response was needed from the teacher, since Jake hadn't decided to take this first draft to publication. Prewriting-drafting was the focus for the week.

Teacher-and-student dialogue continues productively each week through the Writing Cycle with the help of the rubric at the bottom of the student guide. Of this crude rubric, Rick Stiggins notes, "The Writing Cycle's simple system of student self-assessment relates squarely to the conclusions we drew in our research on formative assessment." It is the kind of simple tool that bridges the gap between the standards-based instruction of teachers and the more concrete assessment understood by students and parents: letter and number grades. The standards-based symbols of (◎), (+) and (▭) translate for students and parents as 85 (B), 100 (A) and 70 (D). The result? Students set their sights on exceeding expectations of a standard to earn the A that they want to show off.

That's it. These two pages provide the overview of the nine tasks of the Writing Cycle. The first seven tasks occur in the Working Portfolio (chapters 6–13). Tasks 8 and 9 appear in an Unassisted Writing Sample (chapter 14). When the key features (page 16) and the nine writing tasks (pages 17–18) of the Writing Cycle combine, they create a rigorous routine for empowering students to write throughout the writing process.

I know this charge to complete nine writing tasks in as many weeks with students sounds neither simple nor easy. For you, it means introducing up to six new practices, and none can be left out if you want your students to be the best writers they can. So let the six practices of the Writing Cycle emerge over time, and the way to present each practice will become clear. In this chapter, you saw the Writing Cycle logs support the dialogue between you and your students. In chapter 4, you meet the words that make your dialogue informative, so powerful that it makes the writer's workshop model work with ease. Eight simple words used in talking with your students about their writing make all the difference. The Writing Cycle can become an easy, smooth-flowing framework of productive teaching and learning.

Looking Back

In your response journal, describe two benefits that you already see in the Writing Cycle for you as a teacher in your present classes.

Looking Ahead

What is coming up in your curriculum that will benefit from the use of the Writing Cycle presented in this chapter?

Figure 3.2

Writing Cycle Log *for Teacher Expectations*
An Instructional Guide (Completed by Ms. Song)

Modes of Writing

A **Narration**	G **Explain a problem**	M **Poetry**
B **Description**	H **Explain a process**	N **Summarizing**
C **Character sketch**	I **Explain a solution**	O **Support an opinion/**
D **Imaginative writing**	J **Interpretation**	**solution**
E **Explain a cause/effect**	K **Compare/contrast**	P **Miscellaneous**
F **Explain a classification**	L **Letter**	

Week	Step	Mode	**Expec-tation	Description of Topic	Points
I	*1st Draft #1	C	3 ¶s	Favorite character you've met in reading this year.	85
				(Half of the points are from my prewriting and half from my first draft.)	
II	*1st Draft #2	K	3 ¶s	Compare/contrast yourself with a character from reading	85
III	*1st Draft #3	O	3 ¶s	Support your opinion about a hero from our history book.	85
IV	Revision	O	Three picture sentences	Circle three picture sentences. Then add two or more sentences to each so readers see what you mean.	85
				(A description of how I used this revision strategy in my first draft.)	
V	Proofing	◎		With your proofing trio, correct 3/4 of your errors of capital letters, subject-verb pairs, punctuation, spelling.	85
				(The kind of errors and what percent of them I corrected.)	
VI	Evaluate	+		Support an Opinion Final Evaluation Form (See example on page 146.)	85
				(How close was my estimate or a classmate's estimate of my final grade?)	
VII	Publish	◎		Mount and illustrate your final draft on construction paper from the art closet (extra credit).	5–15
				(A description of how I followed my teacher's publication plan.)	
VIII–IX	Unassisted Writing Sample	◎		Benchmark test for response to literature.	85

*Includes a completed assignment page, word bank and first draft
**Description of what it takes to meet the standard ◎ and earn 85 points

Figure 3.3

Writing Cycle *for Student Self-Check*
A Learning Log

Modes of Writing

A Narration	G Explain a problem	M Poetry
B Description	H Explain a process	N Summarizing
C Character sketch	I Explain a solution	O Support an opinion/
D Imaginative writing	J Interpretation	solution
E Explain a cause/effect	K Compare/contrast	P Miscellaneous
F Explain a classification	L Letter	

Week	Step	Mode	**Self-Check	Description of Topic	Points
I	*1st Draft #1	C	◎	My favorite character is Horrible Harry.	90
				(Half of the points are from my prewriting and half from my first draft.)	
II	*1st Draft #2	K	◎	Muggie Maggie and Alex are very different.	85
III	*1st Draft #3	O	◎	President Abe Lincoln was a wise president	90
IV	Revision	O	+	I circled four sentences and wrote two extra sentences. That is why I give myself an A+	95
				(A description of how I used this revision strategy in my first draft.)	
V	Proofing		◎	Shane and Maia helped me fix most of my mistakes	90
				(The kind of errors and what percent of them I corrected.)	
VI	Evaluate		+	We scored my draft too high.	86
				(How close was my estimate or a classmate's estimate of my final grade?)	
VII	Publish		◎	I taped my final draft on blue construction paper with a copy of Abe Lincoln from our book.	+5
				(A description of how I followed my teacher's publication plan)	
VIII-IX	Unassisted Writing Sample		◎	My response to the literature test.	90

*Includes a completed assignment page, word bank and first draft

Key: + exceeds expectations ◎ meets expectations ⊜ approaches expectations

Chapter 4

Kindling Innate Abilities

Common Core State Standards for Writing

Range and Content of Student Writing—To build a foundation for college and career readiness, students need to learn to use writing as a way of offering and supporting opinions, demonstrating understanding of the subjects they are studying and conveying real and imagined experiences and events. They learn to appreciate that a key purpose of writing is to communicate clearly to an external, sometimes unfamiliar audience, and they begin to adapt the form and content of their writing to accomplish a particular task and purpose. They develop the capacity to build knowledge on a subject through research projects and to respond analytically to literary and informational sources. To meet these goals, students must devote significant time and effort to writing, producing numerous pieces over short and extended time frames throughout the years.

"The words *voice, pictures* and *flow* instead of *style, ideas* and *organization* allow students to easily understand exactly what they need to stay focused on for a great piece of writing. These words stay in their heads when they are writing."

—Donna Knight, grade 5 teacher

Now that you have met the Writing Cycle and are considering putting it into practice, your students have a solid chance of experiencing the "range and content of student writing" of the Common Core. Moreover, the key terms presented in this chapter assure that they arrive there mostly under their own power. You can expect your students to move confidently, understanding that their focused thoughts on what they are learning are sufficient to "develop the capacity to build knowledge on a subject … [from] literary and informational sources." They will learn to trust your well-quantified teacher expectations and "devote significant time and effort to writing, producing numerous pieces over short and extended time frames throughout the years." It all begins with a commonsense shift in the vocabulary of writing for

- Setting the stage for you and your students to write in class.
- Talking about writing with them.

The Writing Cycle builds on Noam Chomsky's language acquisition device (LAD), the powerful, prewired "box" in our minds that makes language learning—spoken or written—possible for us all. Some educators describe the miracle of language learning in humans differently, but they all agree that it requires both innate and environmental conditions. Students come to school capable of learning to write. The Writing Cycle provides the scaffold for supporting students as they explore their inborn ability to acquire written language. It is up to us teachers to talk about writing in ways that keep their minds active in their blossoming LAD.

Eight simple terms help you do precisely that—*voice, pictures, flow, invite, model, write, look* and *learn.* These help you and your students understand yourselves as writers and talk about writing better than any words I know. Your students need not memorize the Common Core State Standards for writing. They need only know that their thoughts contain

> **Voice:** special words that let readers see their full meaning, personality and feelings
> **Pictures** that show the details of their thoughts
> **Flow,** which makes their thoughts easy for others to understand

Use these three words every time you talk writing with your students. Here's why.

The language of writing in most classrooms and textbooks focuses on know-about knowledge of writing. Craft and skill mini-lessons model and teach students about style, ideas, organization and conventions. Since students have trouble with how to write—know-how knowledge—this focus on know-about knowledge isn't much help. That is simply the limitation of the current language of writing. In a nutshell, as you use these eight words to present the Writing Cycle, your students focus on know-how knowledge. That's what it takes to kindle the innate ability to write within all of our students.

So what do teachers of elementary and middle-grade students need to know about writing in order to be the teachers of writing that students need? The answer is, Not as much as they think. In this case, less is better; I remind myself constantly, Talk less; write more. That's why I'm devoting a whole chapter to this message.

The first thing to remember in the less-talk-more-write approach to writing is to establish the right instructional game. In American education, the prevailing game has been, and continues to be, *What Does Teacher Want?* Teachers and students play it in kindergarten. Parents work hard to get their children into the "right" teacher's class. As a graduate student, you probably picked your professors based on their reputation for toughness; I know I did. Students of Flannery O'Connor recall her saying, "Playing *What Does Teacher Want?* is the game that forfeits learning; the game that ensures learning is, *What Am I Thinking?*" As you'll see in Figure 4.1 below, the two instructional games contrast starkly.

In truth, you and I signal the correct instructional game by the words we use to talk about writing with our students, and our students pick up on the signals immediately. The words *style, ideas* and *organization* bring unintended but powerful distractions to students' minds. When I ask students to tell me what is meant by writing style or organization, they sit in silence, wondering what answer I'm fishing for. In addition, *style, ideas* and *organization* make students think of something other than writing, as shown in Figure 4.2 (page 26).

Instead of *style, ideas* and *organization*, use the terms *voice, pictures* and *flow* attributed to the teachings of Flannery O'Connor. *Style, ideas* and *organization* move students outside of their minds as they try to understand knowledge about writing. *Voice, pictures* and *flow* move students inside their heads where authentic writing begins.

Important Synonyms of *Style, Ideas* and *Organization*

The words *style, ideas* and *organization* are not going away; they are deeply embedded in America's conversations about writing, so we must use them. Start teaching writing with voice, pictures and flow, and introduce *style, ideas* and *organization* as words for the same ideas. Use voice, pictures and flow in mini-lessons and work sessions when you want to make sure

Figure 4.1 Comparing Instructional Games

Feature	*What Does Teacher Want?*	*What Am I Thinking?*
Focus	Teacher-centered	Student-centered
Location	Outside of the head	Inside the mind
Emphasis	On the trivial	On the essential
Standard-related	Uncertain	An integral part of the standard
Assessment	Uncertain indicator of learning	Formative assessment of learning
Engagement	Superficial, short-lived	Deep, long-lasting
Overall estimate	A guessing game unrelated to teaching and learning	Students receive full credit for explaining fully what they understand or even misunderstand

Figure 4.2 Traits of Writing

Trait of writing...	makes students think of...
Style	clothing or personal behavior. Most students can point to peers who have style; most do not believe they have it.
Ideas	peers and adults whom they call "smart"; many students find comfort in claiming, "I have no clue." In class they point to the handful of students who have *ideas*.
Organization	habits of health, cleanliness and personal behavior. Students know some peers and adults who are organized; few think that they are.

students write about their own thoughts. At the close of a writing lesson, bring on style, ideas and organization. You'll be delighted by how quickly students embrace and talk about their writing using these terms and how much they help them understand style, ideas and organization.

Voice: Students hear a voice inside their heads as they write. They readily point out the phrases in the writing of others that show personality, emotion and attitude.

Pictures: Students readily acknowledge pictures of their thoughts as they write. As they read or listen to writing, they see pictures in their minds in vivid detail.

Flow: Students can tell you when their writing flows and when it stops flowing. They say their writing flows better from a plan. They instinctively react to writing that does not flow and point to the exact place that the flow stopped.

Voice, pictures and *flow* are always the right words to use with all students, from the most to least experienced, from kindergarten to twelfth grade. I recently met middle-grade students who wrote their opinion of gender-segregated classrooms in letters to their principal. It was time for them to share their first drafts and get help in improving them. They had not used the words *voice, pictures* and *flow* to describe writing before, so I pulled out my chart, found on page 38.

When I randomly paired up PALs* to read their writing aloud to one another, they followed my directions without hesitation. I announced that

---

*Peer-Assisted Learning System, a collection of concrete, specific share and respond strategies that ensure the power of author's chair is experienced by every student on every writing task. Several examples are included in PALS appendix (see page 189). Others need to be created to fit the occasion.

PAL A had 90 seconds to read his first draft to Pal B

PAL B had 60 seconds to
   o Respond to PAL A's writing with the word that stood out in PAL A's writing: *voice, pictures* or *flow*
   o Point to two or three phrases to prove her choice

PAL A wrote the word he heard PAL B say and circled the parts she identified.

As I expected, I heard PALs interact with confidence.

In one set of PALs, PAL A read and PAL B announced without hesitation, "Your writing makes me think of *voice*; you had attitude! You really believe that boys and girls should be in class together." PAL B read her writing aloud to PAL A, and PAL A said, "*Pictures*, I could picture the boys teasing the girls in your math class. Nobody learned very much in that class."

That's the kind of confident interchange I hear in the voices of students the first time they use the concepts of voice, pictures and flow.

In response to an elementary student's narration of an event that ended with a scar, "Tony's story made me see a picture of blood and scratches when he crashed his bike [picture]." In a persuasive essay for choosing the local homeless shelter as a class project, "I agreed with Wo Kim's opinion. It was strong, almost scary. Her words made me feel sorry for homeless people [voice]." In an expository report of how a student did something well, "I see the steps of how Jose builds bird houses. I could follow his writing and build one, too, maybe [flow]."

In *The Myth of Laziness* (2002), Melvin Levine poignantly describes the benefits of writing for students when the writing is a direct outcome of their thoughts, not some formulaic guess of that their teachers want:

> By writing, a kid learns to mesh multiple brain functions, and ultimately writing is something you need to do whatever you do to earn a living. In a sense, the act of writing helps build and maintain the brain pathways that connect diverse functions, such as language memory and motor control. In other words, writing is a way for a kid to practice getting his act together. Writing also serves as a platform for systematic thinking and a means of problem solving, two more abilities needed in any career (pp. 7–8).

Script for Introducing Voice, Pictures and Flow

Sometimes a more deliberate introduction of these terms applies. The following routine works for me every time I meet a new group of students. Students move easily from *What Does Teacher Want?* to *What Am I Thinking?* I begin.

"Before we start writing together, I want to make sure that we think about writing the same way. So take out a clean sheet of paper and write the three words I'm writing on the board on the first, fifth and tenth lines of your paper."

[I space out *voice*, *pictures* and *flow* on the board.]

Question 1: "Write this question to the right of *voice*: 'Are there voices when you write?'"

[Everyone usually writes out the sentence fully; some ask if they are doing it the right way.]

Most often, no one risks an answer to this unusual question, so I add, "I'm waiting for an answer. Someone tell me if there are voices when you write?" Here are a range of typical responses:

"Oh no, we're not supposed to talk when we write."

"I don't know."

"Oh yes, you can hear Ms. Howard's class talking through the wall right there."

[I don't challenge these perceptions, but move to a version of the same question.]

"How about voices you can hear when you are all alone without a person, computer, iPod or TV within earshot?"

[Be patient until a student admits that he hears voices in his head. Sometimes students simply tap the sides of their head with their index finger.]

I usually have a little fun with the right-responder and ask, "Who are the voices talking to?" When the student replies, "me," I continue the fun. "So you talk to yourself when you write?" Since the students laugh at this admission, I quickly announce that all writers talk to themselves inside their heads when they write. That's precisely how all writers write!

Question 2: "Write this question to the right of the word pictures: 'Are there pictures when you write?'"

[Students usually say "yes" this time, so I continue.]

"So where is the picture when you start writing?" I ask them to draw and fill in the three boxes on their own paper, following my model on the board. The picture

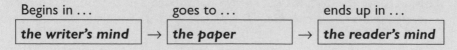

Begins in . . .   goes to . . .   ends up in . . .

| the writer's mind | → | the paper | → | the reader's mind |

The final point is critical: "So who is responsible for making certain that the picture in the reader's mind resembles the picture in the writer's mind?"

[When the students agree that the writer is responsible, I know the shift to *What am I thinking?* is complete.]

Question 3: "Write the third question to the right after the word *flow*: 'Is there flow when you write?'"

[By this time, students are talkative, ready to cite examples of flow and lack of flow in writing, "When you have to stop to figure some words out, the writing isn't flowing." They say this like it should be obvious to everyone in the room, and indeed it should.]

"How right you are. On many state writing rubrics," I point out, "*voice* is the same as the trait of style and counts for 20% of the total score. The word *pictures* is called *ideas* and counts for 40% of the total score. *Flow* corresponds to *organization*, roughly 20% of the total score. I hereby declare that we are on the same page. We are ready to write."

A caveat: the next time you and your students write, many of them will revert to playing *What Does Teacher Want?* The game is deeply engrained in the psyche of U.S. students. Be patient. Continued use of voice, pictures and flow moves them confidently toward strong habits of playing *What Am I Thinking?* Eventually, they will play the right game all the time. It is only a matter of time. And be aware that what you say might trigger the old game *What Does Teacher Want?*—like saying "very good" when students share their writing aloud. It's easy to do; at first I did it often. I'll point out places where that can easily happen in chapters to come.

To *voice*, *pictures* and *flow*, add a sequence of five words that ease the task of keeping students focused on what they are thinking. These words frame each mini-lesson, work session and author's chair close. The first, *invite* and *model*, refine and sharpen the focus of mini-lessons.

Invite **students to write along with you.** This is very different from prompting students to write and then finding time to write along with them. You take the lead by writing. Sit down and show intense engagement in writing exactly what you asked your students to write. I used to prompt students to write and move around the room, trying to motivate the slower ones to get started; now I invite, sit down and write, and they all follow, each at his or her own pace.

Model	the focused strategy of the mini-lesson in your own writing. When introducing a genre, share your writing in the assigned genre, even if it is on a different topic. Second best is model writing of former students or teachers known to your students. Point to examples of the genre in the writing of authors whom students have read in literature. But don't expect professional models to deliver the impact of models from you, former students or well-known colleagues.

The third word is *write* and includes quantified expectations of length, key terms and time. Then students readily self-assess the degree to which they reached or exceeded your expectations. Without the quantified expectations of the word *write*, work sessions can easily become downtimes for students' minds instead of a string of one engaged moment after another.

Write	the writing task prompted in the mini-lesson, using the specific strategy modeled. After you write yourself for 1 or 2 minutes, move about the room to provide one-on-one assistance to students as needed.

Words four and five are *look* and *learn*. Without an emphasis on *look* and *learn*, the author's chair can become a rote routine deadened through habits of comments like, "I like your details," "Tell me more about X," "You used lots of details," or "You used big words again."

Look	for and point out concrete, specific features of writing in a PALs-shared writing. PAL A shares her writing; PAL B says that her voice, pictures or flow stood out in her writing and identifies two or three examples. See the PALS appendix for additional strategies.
Learn	the elements and benefits of each new writing task with every group of students. This step seems repetitious, but it is critical for students new to your instruction. Ask your class to help you list them for all to see. As you write on an interactive board, the students record their version of the list in their writing notebook.

To keep the author's chair alive and productive, I present it in different forms in the course of a month.

- **Daily PALS.** In the last 7 to 10 minutes of writing instruction, PALs huddle to hear each other read their writing aloud and record their responses to one another's writing. PALs stay together for only two weeks; students need to experience an ever-expanding audience.

- **Weekly small groups.** Each Friday, students meet to read their writing to the group and record the responses to the writing of others on cards you provide.
- **Monthly whole group (a rotation on a Friday).** Students meet as a whole group to listen to the writing of selected peers and respond with a rubric or checklist projected for all to see.

The Writing Cycle framework energized by eight simple terms—*voice, pictures, flow, invite, model, write, look* and *learn*—extends Donald Murray's invitation in *The Craft of Writing* to "write with me." The details of each lesson of *Writer's Workshop for the Common Core* makes it easy to take full advantage of Murray's sage advice. For example, week 1 of the Writing Cycle focuses on prewriting and drafting.

Monday, your mini-lesson invites students to prewrite with you, following a model that you have written.

Tuesday, you take 7 to 10 minutes of the writing time to coach students who need help reaching your expectations for prewriting. Other students get a head start on the word study (Marzano 2005) or sentence study (Combs 2011) of the day.

Wednesday, invite students to write a first draft with you based on their prewriting plans.

Thursday, take 7 to 10 minutes of writing time to coach students who need help completing their first drafts. Other students move directly to word study or sentence study.

Friday, select students to read their first drafts aloud in four small groups of six or seven. Each small group selects one draft to share with the whole class in an author's chair in front of the appropriate rubric projected behind them. Peers use the language of the rubric to identify

- Two ways the writing meets or exceeds the standard.
- Two ways the writing could be improved.

So push aside the pressure to talk *about* writing. Relax and enjoy yourself as you invite your students to write with you. Don't be anxious about knowing what to teach about the writing genre you prompt. Students will learn more from watching you in the act of writing and watching your progress than they could ever learn from you in direct instruction about the writing process. Once the prompt of a mini-lesson is in play, the simple framework of invite, model, write, look and learn clicks in. This sequence is boxed for your convenience in chapters 6 through 13.

I'm eager for you to see the huge difference those eight words of the Writing Cycle make in the performance of students. The next chapter starts with a snapshot of students in a Writing Cycle class who introduced themselves as voice-writers, picture-writers and flow-writers. It concludes with the widespread impact of those eight words of the Writing Cycle on tests of written expression.

Looking Back

In your response journal, explain the benefits using voice, pictures and flow—instead of style, content and organization—in referring to traits of writing. What benefit do you see for students?

Looking Ahead

At what point coming up in your curriculum do you see an opportunity to introduce voice, pictures and flow? Which of the two explanations of the terms do you find better suited to you?

Chapter 5

The Difference the Writing Cycle Makes

Common Core State Standards for Writing

Each year in their writing, students should demonstrate increasing sophistication in all aspects of language use, from vocabulary and syntax to the development and organization of ideas, and they should address increasingly demanding content and sources. Students advancing through the grades are expected to meet each year's grade-specific standards and retain or further develop skills and understandings mastered in preceding grades. The expected growth in student writing ability is reflected both in the standards themselves and in the collection of annotated student writing samples.

"From the lowest-performing school out of eleven elementary schools in our district to the highest in one year, our students' writing is advancing."

—Dr. Martha Taylor, principal

I have shown you how the Writing Cycle emerged to ease the use of the writer's workshop model. If you have already introduced your students to voice, pictures and flow in writing, you have also started experiencing this ease. Of course, the difference that the Writing Cycle makes has to be more than easy; it must improve student mastery of their writing process in class as well as their performance on tests of written expression. Administrators like Dr. Taylor believe that the Writing Cycle framework for pacing writer's workshop has their schools on mark for effective writing. Look with me at a classroom that employs the Writing Cycle faithfully. Then review student performance data on independent assessments of written expression.

Admittedly, I invited myself to visit a fifth-grade class of writers at Woodstation Elementary School, a half hour south of Chattanooga, Tennessee. The teacher, Ms. Knight, was an engaged participant in a Writer's Workshop for the Common Core workshop. Through e-mail exchanges, I sensed that she was implementing the strategies of the Writing Cycle with intention and care. Even though I called to invite myself, she invited me to drop by and meet her students, and I accepted.

She graciously introduced me to her second-period class. "This is Dr. Combs, the man you have seen on the DVD and the author of the Writing Cycle that is making you terrific writers." I blushed and nodded as the students clapped their welcome and opened my mouth to say a few appreciative words, but I heard Ms. Knight continue.

"Dr. Combs, my class would like to introduce themselves to you as well. Will all of my voice-writers please stand?"

Since this is the kind of introduction I recommend in every workshop, I smiled and saw eight students stand up next to their desks with eager eyes and broad, toothy smiles. They said nothing, and I knew it was my turn to speak.

"Is that so? Voice-writers, indeed." I paused to think of exactly what to say next. "Will one of you show me how this is so?"

Instead of students' heads swiveling this way and that with grins that dared someone to make the first move, three students slipped their hands into their desks and produced a current Working Portfolio for the persuasive genre. The boy closest to me had his portfolio open to a first draft well ahead of the others, so I asked his name and the topic.

"I'm Joseph, sir. We had to write a letter to an adult and convince them we were old enough to do something we hadn't done before."

"And what did you think you were old enough to do?"

"To have my own cell phone. You want to hear it?"

Of course I did, and before I could say another word his draft was out and in position to read. Fortunately, Ms. Knight had conditioned him to let the teacher set a response pattern for the class before he read a first draft, so I spoke on cue. "We'll let Joseph read, and then we'll see if his writing radiates voice. Three volunteers will mention whether it was the voice, pictures or the flow in his writing that was most noticeable. Who will volunteer?" A dozens hands shot up, and I selected two girls and a boy. I nodded to Joseph who read with gestured animation.

Dear mom,

I believe that I am old enough to have a cell phone because all of the other kids have one. What if something happens? I need it in case of a visit to a friend's house. Mom, I'm absolutely serious, A-L-L of the other kids have one. I'm like the only one that doesn't. You've got to know HOW that makes a person feel. So if you agree with me, stop reading here . . .

Okay, apparently you didn't stop reading, so here's my other begging reason why I should have a cell phone—in case of an emergency, and you know how often kids have emergencies. I mean like what happens when I am locked out of the house or I am stuck in a building that is catching on fire. A cell phone means "911" is one key-stroke away. I'll let you think about this picture of me in some disaster . . . and, of course, you can stop reading if you agree.

"Whoa, Joseph," I said. "From the looks on your classmate's faces, I think they have already made a decision about our response."

I pointed to the three volunteer responders who each said "voice" in quick succession. One responder said that "A-L-L of the other kids" demonstrated Joseph's voice; a second mentioned, "Okay, apparently you didn't stop reading, so"; a third, "I'm absolutely serious." I watched Joseph; he had pulled out a pencil and circled the phrases mentioned and marked them with a *V.* Ms. Knight had conditioned this class to a well-defined author's chair routine. They didn't have to be in a chair or in a section of the room for the rigorous routine of share-respond to apply. When asked, the class said "voice" unanimously.

Note that Joseph skipped over the opening paragraph in his first draft, diving headlong into a body paragraph with overpowering voice or style. He trusted Ms. Knight when she advised students to write what they were thinking, even if that meant getting down to the reasons in a persuasive draft with passion. Henry David Thoreau advised all writers to "write while the heat is in you." That was definitely true for Joseph. Later, in his revision, he crafted an introductory paragraph displayed on a writer's block display board. He knew how to approach his mother, like so many other fifth graders: he complimented her profusely and stated that his life had gotten to a point that something had to change. He needed a cell phone.

Mrs. Knight's introductions of her students continued; eleven stood up as picture writers; seven stood up as flow writers. I was obviously the only one in the room who didn't know who was what kind of writer. A picture writer and the flow writer convinced me that they were rightly placed, so I asked, "This is remarkable; you all know which group you are in! How?"

"That's easy," came a reply. "Somebody tells us every time we read aloud in author's chair."

What a dream! Fifth-graders who understood that all writing consists of voice (style), pictures (ideas) and flow (organization), and that their personal profile as a writer tilts in one of these three directions. I didn't know this about my writing until graduate school.

Ms. Knight continued with the lesson: a Framed Draft for 1st Draft #2 to emphasize the use of concrete, specific details in the structure and scope of a persuasive essay (Figure 5.1). Without a cue, the remaining students took out their Working Portfolios and turned to the Writing Cycle Log for Student Self-Check. They logged the date and mode of writing. Then they

Figure 5.1 People Have Fun in Cities

Read through the following draft expressively, saying "blank" at every blank. Words that fit in the blanks will come to your mind as you read. You will see it is a frame for a first draft. On a clean sheet of lined paper, begin copying the frame up to the point of the first blank. Then add at least the minimum number of words (three, five or seven). Use small function words such as *on, beside, that, at, from* or *with* to help you reach the minimum. The more words you add, the more the frame will become your own, and the prouder you will be.

People live and work in cities, but they also find time for fun. Cities have large parks to _____. Companies provide places to _____. Some places are _____ because they have _____ to see.

looked up to read the writing topic prompt on the interactive board for the mini-lesson.

Using A Working Portfolio like the model at www.writingtowin.com, they turned to page 5 to complete My Assignment Page, then page 6 for The Word Bank to Support an Opinion before drafting their version of the Framed Draft in their Working Portfolios on pages 7 through 8.

Within 15 minutes, two students had finished their first drafts and moved over to the designated author's chairs to read and respond in PALS to each other's drafts. When the 20 minutes for the work session was over, the remaining students had PAL-ed up and shared their work in turn, following a specific PALS strategy. As one PAL shared, the other wrote on a response card one thing that was strong about the writing and a question that came to mind. As each PAL finished, the pairs signaled Ms. Knight, and she spoke: "There's time for two people to share with whole group. Stacie and Tucker, we haven't heard from you in a while."

A volunteer responded to Stacie's first draft without prompting. "She usually is a voice writer, but today she made me see really clear pictures." A second student concurred. "She used words like *dressed in bright colors* and *walked fast in hordes of people.* I see why she'll never live in a big city." A third questioned her. "How come you don't want to live in a city? You love shopping in Chattanooga."

Stacie's response? "Chattanooga isn't big; it's just medium. I like it a lot." That seemed to satisfy all concerned.

I noticed that a smile had developed on my face. Not every class I visit has the routines for writing this deeply ingrained; I know this. However, when teachers implement the routines of the Writing Cycle with fidelity, strong, independent writers emerge. Teachers have more time to write along with their students. Clearly, Ms. Knight and her students were approaching peak-performance writing, but I needed to hear it from her students.

So in my most naïve tone, I asked, "So what's with all this writing without asking Ms. Knight what she wants?"

"We're writing what we're thinking; that's the way we write in here," came a response from somewhere.

"You mean that you use Framed Drafts for writing all of the time?" I asked.

"No, sir," from a different voice, "we did a narrative Framed Draft before and an informational one."

I continued, "So there's not a difference in Framed Drafts?"

The same voice responded, "Sure there is. One has story details, one has opinion details, and today was explaining details." That seemed to satisfy the speaker and those around her. It satisfied me.

"Does this mean that all the writing you have done this year has details that make pictures in readers' minds?" I prodded. "Does all writing everywhere have pictures?"

"Yes?" said an impatient voice. "Writing is writing. It all makes pictures in your head. See?" The student pointed to a bulletin board chart displayed prominently in the line of sight of all the students.

"Yeah, it's just the way we write in here," a final voice said conclusively.

Ms. Knight succeeded at planting the key ideas of the Writing Cycle in her students. Writing is all about voice, pictures and flow. She had a chart posted that defined voice, one that defined pictures and one that defined flow in plain sight (see Figure 5.2, page 38). Her students knew these words well, and they knew how to put them to work in their writing.

Three teachers new to the Writing Cycle framework put it this way.

- "For the first time in teaching writing, my students are working harder than I am. The Writing Cycle prompts students to make key choices at each step of the writing process without my reminding them one or several times."
- "All twenty-six students of my 'disadvantaged' students met or exceeded the target on our state's Grade 5 Writing Assessment in 2010. I just used the Working Portfolio and Unassisted Writing Sample like you showed us." Later she explained, "I was going to retire at the end of this year, but teaching writing has become too much fun. It's a joy to see the students take control of their writing and work with confidence. I'll see you next year."
- "I'd never quite figured out what to do to help my gifted students understand and appreciate the writing process. This initiative just

Figure 5.2 Defining Voice, Pictures and Flow

Use your voice.	Show atmosphere, attitude, confidence, conviction, disposition, emotion, energy, feeling, frame of mind, humor, individuality, manner, mood, nature, novelty, passion, personality, pitch, point of view, precision, sensation, temper (good or bad), tone and uniqueness.
Make pictures ...	... to bare, bring to light, clarify, demonstrate, describe, depict, detail, disclose, display, establish, exemplify, exhibit, explain, explicate, expose, flesh out, give details, illustrate, make clear, portray, prove, represent, reveal, show, show evidence of, stage, substantiate, tell all and uncover.
Let thoughts flow ...	... to arrange, assemble, associate, attach, blend in, combine, connect, coordinate, correlate, gift wrap, join, link up, organize, package, position, put in order, put together, relate, shape and smooth out.

clicked. The strategies resemble what I was already doing, but the Writing Cycle just gives students more responsibility, and they go for it."

I've seen these teachers in action; they are helping students in important and long-lasting ways. As warming as these opinions are, they need data. Without data, we are just a collection of happy teachers of writing with glowing opinions.

In our experience with the Writing Cycle, the scores on tests of written expressions spike upward upon the completion of the first Writing Cycle. In the *2010 Action Research Report of the Writing Cycle,* the results for grades 5 and 8 speak for themselves. Figure 5.3 on page 39 shows those results.

Moore Elementary is a largely African American school in Griffin, Georgia, a former mill town in central Georgia an hour south of Atlanta. The fifth-grade teachers who used writer's workshop saw the Writing Cycle one day after school in December. Their principal said that if they committed to using the Working Portfolio and Unassisted Writing Sample in their lessons, she would buy them for each student. They did, and she did. Fifth-grade students' scores moved Moore Elementary from the bottom-performing to top-performing elementary school in its district.

Figure 5.3 Results Before and After the Writing Cycle

Grade	School	Prior to the Writing Cycle		Writing Cycle, Year One		Change
		Pass Rate	District Rank	Pass Rate	District Rank	
5	Moore ES	68%	11 of 11	87%	1 of 11	+19%
5	Redan ES	49%	82 of 84	67%	42 of 84	+18%
5	Southside ES	73%	5 of 6	88%	1 of 6	+15%
5	Joseph Martin ES	87%	3 of 8	93%	1 of 8	+ 6%
5	Georgia	78%		73%		− 5%
3-5	Iva ES	21%	3 of 3	82%	1 of 3	+61%
3-5	South Carolina	74%		76%		+ 2%
8	Collegedale MS		4.51 of 6.0		4.88 of 6.0	+ .37
8	Tennessee		4.21		4.18	− .03
8	Newbern MS	46%	3 of 3	83%	1 of 3	+37%
8	E. Columbus MA	63%	10 of 13	78%	2 of 13	+15%
6	Georgia	78%		73%		− 5%

Southside Elementary is one of six rural schools with a record of respectible scores on state writing tests. Southside students ranked fifth out of the six schools, equivalent with its student demographics—that is, until the Writing Cycle packets made their appearance. The sibling schools noted what Southside was doing and are renewing their commitment to the Writing Cycle. Redan Elementary posted a similar rise in student performance, but with suburban African American students. Its teachers had time to complete Writing Cycles in persuasive and expository genres prior to the Grade 5 Writing Assessment. In a single year, a bottom-performing school (eighty-second out of eighty-four elementary schools) moved up to the forty-second position, a jump that has the attention of their district leaders. Joseph Martin Elementary (JMES) is a racially balanced school of middle-class students that has had the highest writing scores out of eight elementary schools in its district. When two district schools initiated the Writing Cycle model and moved ahead of JMES students, JMES implemented the Writing Cycle itself and regained the top-performing place, with 23% of the students exceeding the state standard. (Who questions the benefits of a little friendly competition?)

Middle schools using the Writing Cycle framework post similar results. Two city schools in Valdosta and Columbus, Georgia, posted scores that moved them from the bottom to top-performing in their respective districts. The data tell the story. Action research studies in Georgia elementary schools clearly show that the use of the Writing Cycle framework transfers the sound principles of teaching writing to student performance on independent tests of written expression. There is no need to stop using writer's workshop and teach the test a month prior to test time.

In South Carolina and Tennessee, additional action research data corroborate these findings. In three years, a bottom-performing, 95% white, rural school in western South Carolina saw the percent of its fifth-graders who met and exceeded state standards rise from 21% to over 80%. In a suburban Chattanooga school with a 90% white population, the mean score out of a possible 6.0 on the Tennessee Comprehensive Assessment Program (T-CAP) achievement tests for writing rose from 4.51 in 2009 to 4.88 in 2010. The number of students who posted perfect scores of 6.0 increased from 6 in 2009 to 12 in 2010, 22% of the 55 test takers. By contrast, the school system in the county posted a mean score of 4.1 with 1% perfect scores, while the state registered a mean score of 4.2 with 2% perfect scores. In three states with different independent instruments of writing assessment, faithful implementation of the Writing Cycle moved large numbers of students from "did not meet" to "meets" state standards. In addition, schools with students who met state standards moved in significant numbers to exceeding state standards. While teachers admit that teaching writing with the Writing Cycle is still not a simple undertaking, faithful implementation of it makes teaching the writing process the easiest that it has ever been for them and their students. (Data is not yet available on the Common Core State Standards, but we expect that the results will be strong since the Writing Cycle correlates well to the CCSS.)

The remaining chapters spell out exactly how the Writing Cycle makes such a difference. Over the next nine chapters, observe how the framework of the Writing Cycle clearly focuses on each of six widely accepted traits of writing: ideas (chapters 6–11), organization (chapters 6, 7 and 10), sentence fluency (chapters 8 and 11), voice (chapters 6–11) word choice (chapters 8–11) and conventions (chapter 12). Meet a systematic way to provide students choice within the context of the Common Core State Standards (Reeves). Experience a simple system for student self-assessment that sparks insightful reflection on every writing task (Stiggins). See the benefits of setting a gently accelerated pace for moving through the writing process (Sousa). Change up the pace of rigorous writing with refreshing word and sentence studies (Marzano and Graham). In short, welcome to classes of writers in which students work just as hard as their teachers—and maybe even harder.

Looking Back

In your response journal, describe two features of the exemplary Writing Cycle classroom that you believe already apply to you as a teacher in your present classes.

Looking Ahead

What is coming up in your curriculum that will benefit from two features like the ones you gleaned from this chapter?

Chapter 6

Analyze a Writing Topic Prompt with Me

Common Core State Standards for Writing

Text Types and Purposes—2. Write informative/explanatory texts to examine and convey complex ideas and information clearly and accurately through the effective selection, organization and analysis of content.

Production and Distribution of Writing—4. Produce clear and coherent writing in which the development, organization and style are appropriate to task, purpose and audience.

"The most powerful thing a teacher can say is 'write with me.'"

—Donald Murray

Prewriting for first drafts includes two ready-made instructional tools: My Assignment Page and a word bank. The first requires students to focus on the writing topic prompt and documents their understanding. The second transitions their focus from the prompt to a plan for their first draft. For the purposes of this book, My Assignment Page appears in this chapter, and the word bank in chapter 7. In practice, however, students move from one to the other seamlessly.

To help students develop a sense of what makes a good writing topic, provide model writing topic prompts every time they write. Once they are familiar with topic prompts based on state standards for their grade level, they can be expected to start developing their own. So launch the Writing Cycle with a description of the writing topic prompt for 1st Draft #1 on your Writing Cycle Log for Teacher Expectations Wall Chart (page 43).

On the Writing Cycle Log for Student Self-Check (page 44), students log the modes of writing for their first three first drafts and nothing more. They leave the "Description of Topic" blank until they have written their first drafts. Once they have completed 1st Draft #1, prompt them to return to enter the "Description of Topic" based on their individual first draft.

Figure 6.1

Beginning Date: <u>October 10</u>

End Date: <u>December 2</u>

Writing Cycle Log for Teacher Expectations
A Project of the Writing Process

Modes of Writing

A Narration	G Explain a problem	M Poetry
B Description	H Explain a process	N Summarizing
C Character sketch	I Explain a solution	O Support an opinion/
D Imaginative writing	J Interpretation	solution
E Explain a cause/effect	K Compare/contrast	P Miscellaneous
F Explain a classification	L Letter	

Step	Mode	**Expec-tation	Description of Topic	Points
*1st Draft #1	K	4 ¶s	Favorite character you've met in reading this year	85
			(Half of the points are from my prewriting and half from my first draft.)	
*1st Draft #2	K	4 ¶s	Helping a friend choose between two pets for a gift	85
*1st Draft #3	C	4 ¶s	A person who has been influential to me	85

*Includes a completed assignment page, word bank and first draft

** Description of what it takes to meet the standard ◉ and earn 85 points

The plan for My Assignment Page fits into the first two days, as shown in Figure 6.3 (page 45).

Provide students with an overview of the first two days of the week.

Monday: The week's writing task: write 1st Draft #1 in response to a writing topic prompt after completing My Assignment Page and a word bank.

Tuesday: Word study (except students tutored on the use of their word banks).

Mini-Lesson with Scripting for My Assignment Page

INVITE
Interpret the Writing Topic Prompts with Me.

Teacher: **Work on a writing topic prompt with me.** I see from reading your pretest writing samples that you all had different ideas about what the topic meant. Your first drafts show features like some of my first drafts. You read the topic and started writing so quickly that you missed some of the parts of the topic. We can fix this habit in short

Figure 6.2

Name: Khalil Mehta

Beginning Date: October 12

End Date: December 4

Writing Cycle Log *for Student Self-Check*
A Project of the Writing Process

Modes of Writing

A Narration	**G** Explain a problem	**M** Poetry
B Description	**H** Explain a process	**N** Summarizing
C Character sketch	**I** Explain a solution	**O** Support an opinion/ solution
D Imaginative writing	**J** Interpretation	**P** Miscellaneous
E Explain a cause/effect	**K** Compare/contrast	
F Explain a classification	**L** Letter	

Step	Mode	**Self-Check	Description of Topic	Points
*1st Draft #1	⊬	___	_____	___
*1st Draft #2	⊬	___	_____	___
*1st Draft #3	C	___	_____	___

* Includes a completed assignment page, word bank and first draft

**Key: + exceeds expectations ◎ meets expectations ▭ missses expectations

order with My Assignment Page. It helps you slow down and write out your thoughts about the topic so you and I can see when you are on the right track or need some help. Sounds like a useful page, don't you think? Someone read aloud the writing topic prompt for us all to follow along.

Writing Situation

You have been invited by relatives to visit them on the holiday of the year that you like the least. You know that people enjoy getting out on holidays they like and staying home on ones they don't like. Which holidays are your most and least favorite?

Directions for Writing

Write a letter to your relatives explaining that you cannot visit them on the holiday they have invited you to spend with them. Contrast and compare the holiday with one you like the most. Explain that you will be glad to visit them on a holiday that you enjoy.

Figure 6.3 My Assignment Page: 1st Draft #1 of a Writing Cycle Based on a Genre

Mini-lesson—**M L** (7–10 min); work time—**W** (15–20 min); close—**C** (7–10 min)

Day →		Monday	Tuesday
Working Portfolio: 1st Draft # 1	M L	**Invite and Model** **My Assignment Page** and word bank	Small-group conference Word study strategy for others: analogies

	W	**Whole group**
		
		Do **My Assignment Page** (5 min).
		
		Look and Learn **Two students share.**
		
		Do the word bank (15 min).
		
		   *Brainstorm possible topics.
		
		   *Jot list one topic.
		
		Teacher identifies students with incomplete word banks for a small-group conference on Tuesday.
			Word study (PALS)
			
			   Three analogies based on a current science standard.
			
			   Three analogies based on a current ELA standard.

	C	Author's chair close (7–10 min) Look and Learn Students share their completed word bank in PALS or with a small group or the whole group to receive coaching. Listening students mention two strengths and one question about the author's writing.	

I have found no better way to see how well students understand a topic than to have them complete the five items on My Assignment Page. The name of the page sounds ordinary, but it delivers extra-ordinary power. When students complete My Assignment Page as prompted, they prewrite with full engagement. These steps make students see My Assignment Page as a natural thing to do, and student responses to the item tell you how well they understand the writing topic prompt.

- **Quantify your expectations for the five items on an assignment page.** Say, "Someone read the statement in the gray bar at the bottom of the page." (The bar says, "For My Assignment page, earn 20 points for writing a complete sentence for each of these five items.") Students now see that 20 of the possible 100 points for 1st Draft #1 come from this page. Without these 20 points, it will be difficult for them to meet the standard (i.e., earn a B). The twenty points come from how much of the standard they have completed and what remains for them to complete.

Note: At first we thought students needed to choose their topic before they thought about matters of audience and tone, but we discovered that this is not the case. Considering possible audiences and appropriate tone actually helps them zero in on a suitable topic.

- **Show students your completed assignment page based on the topic prompt.** When I modeled this page for this topic prompt, I used "my Aunt Minnie Mae Farris" as my audience and "formal" and "gloomy" as descriptions of my tone. Students have never copied my choices.
- **The first time through My Assignment Page, talk the class through each item, setting (and sticking to) 60 to 90 seconds per item.** In my experience, My Assignment Page takes 10 to 12 minutes to complete the first time with guidance, but 5 to 7 minutes or less on subsequent uses. Your role will shift from guide to monitor.

Note that the teacher model of My Assignment Page (page 47) is one that students are not likely to copy or imitate.

> **DO**
>
> Describe the topic, audience, purpose, tone and rubric of the current topic.

Khalil completed his version of his teacher's model that showed expression of authentic thought. He is definitely not copying his teacher's model (see page 48).

Notice that Khalil's largest and most prominent handwriting on the page is the 20 points that he awarded himself for writing five informative sentences. We can see that he has locked onto the topic prompt and understands it accurately.

My Assignment Page does not always operate without a hitch. Some students skimp on the information they include. This happens in two ways:

- Some writers see My Assignment Page as busywork since they have never been required to take this step before. I like how one teacher responded to a gifted writer who jotted down one to three words per item and printed 20 points in large hand at the top of the page. When she reviewed his page, she said, "Eric, I see you've self-assessed 20 points, without a single sentence on the page. Can you explain that to me."

  "Aw, Mrs. Newsome," Eric moaned, "You're not really going to make me [a self-described talented writer] write complete sentences, are you? That's Mickey Mouse!"

MODEL	**Figure 6.4 Teacher Model**	
Review a completed Assignment Page on a previous topic.	**My Assignment Page:**	1st Draft #3
	Topic:	I'm explaining to a relative why she or he needs to invite me over on my most favorite holiday, not my least favorite one.
	Audience:	I will probably choose my Aunt Minnie Mae Farris.
	Purpose:	My purpose is to explain how I see two holidays very differently.
	Tone:	The tone of my writing will be formal and gloomy.
	Evaluation:	My final draft of this paper, should I choose to revise it, will be scored by a student and a fellow teacher using a Compare and Contrast rubric.

I thrilled at Mrs. Newsome's response, "Oh no, Eric. You misunderstand. I'm not requiring you to write sentences; you may even choose to write nothing at all. But I do insist that you assess yourself accurately. Let's see. What does the gray bar at the bottom of the page say exactly?"

With this question, Eric sighed, put his independent reading book in his desk, took out his pencil and fleshed out five fully informative sentences that helped him off to a better start.

Note: Don't take students' resistance personally; let the bar at the bottom of the page be the bad guy (that's me). The 20 points are just how My Assignment Page works. We see very few blank pages when we stick to the expectation of full, informative sentences.

- Some writers see the expectation of five complete sentences and serve up five completely uninformative ones. For this group of students we turn to PALS. The most workable example is described by Graham and Saddler (2005). Most simply, they suggest that PALs be of different abilities, but not greatly different.* Whenever students are introduced to a new learning task like My Assignment Page, the teacher guides students as a whole group, modeling the completion of the task fully. The second time students use My Assignment Page, the PALs coach each other through the task. PAL A coaches PAL B in completing the first item; PAL B coaches PAL A in completing the second one, and so on.

Figure 6.5 Student Sample

My Assignment Page: 1st Draft #3

20 points

The topic assigned to me:	I will compare and contrast my best and worst holidays.
Audience (Whom am I writing to?):	I get to choose a relative for my audience. It will be someone that likes letters from me.
The purpose of my writing (genre):	I will explain that I can't visit on a holiday I don't like very much.
Tone (serious, humorous, asking, demanding .... Use two descriptive words):	The tone of my paper will be truthful and maybe a little bit funny.
How will my final draft be evaluated? List the title of final evaluation form:	My teacher will use a rubric. It is called Compare and Contrast.

> For My Assignment Page, earn 20 points by writing a complete sentence for each of these five items.

When two students in a pair finish My Assignment Page, one of them signals to the teacher that they are ready to move on.

*Rank order the writers in a class from most to least capable on a reliable index (such as a score on a benchmark writing sample). In a class of twenty-eight, list them from one through twenty-eight on a single page, cut the paper in half between the fourteenth- and fifteenth-ranked student and place the two halves side by side. The first and fifteenth students match up and become PALs, the second and sixteenth become PALs, and so forth. The PALs are of different writing abilities, but not too different.

A note about student-friendly rubrics: Page 50 presents a student-friendly scoring rubric for Compare and Contrast (see also www.eyeon-education.com for a downloadable version). It is based on a state rubric for informational genre, adapted by a group of classroom teachers and refined in a series of test trials. For additional rubrics, see the companion series, *A Writing Cycle for Writer's Workshop* (2011, pp. E-18–E-34).

When the students have finished My Assignment Page, it is time to ask: "How many felt your writing flow as you responded to each of these five items?"

Of the several who raise their hands, select two to share their responses aloud to the entire class. For example, the teacher would say, "Lakisha and Won Mo, just say 'topic' and read your first sentence, 'audience' and read your second sentence, and so on. The rest of us have equally important jobs. I'll call on several of you to mention a strength and a question about the sentences. So listen as Lakisha shares first."

Once the sharing and responding is complete, bring closure to the lesson by letting the students help you list the benefits of My Assignment Page. One list of benefits looked like this. The first item on the list usually appears first.

"We get to give ourselves 20 points for completing the page."
"It makes sure we know the topic."
"Choosing a tone was cool."
"I like the rubric. It tells me how to get a good grade."
"It lets you [the teacher] know if we need help."

Student Self-Assessment: Students complete their work on My Assignment Page by counting up the points they have earned—4 points for each complete, informative sentence. After students complete My Assignment Page with the whole class, they score themselves immediately upon writing the five sentences. Remind them to think ahead. When they earn 20 out of 20 points for My Assignment Page, they are exceeding expectations for 1st Draft #1 (100% of the possible points). When they complete four sentences, they are on target (◎) or 80 points (16 out of 20 converts to 80%). When they complete only three sentences, they missed the target, and at 60% their performance level is failing.

Conclusion: Ask students to respond to the statement, "Writing full sentences in My Assignment Page helps you to think better than if you did the thinking without writing." Help students conclude something like this: "My Assignment Page makes it possible for us to explore what we are thinking more than we do any other way. It reminds us of the quote, 'I never know what I know until I read what I wrote' attributed to writers such as Flannery O'Connor and Ernest Hemingway."

Figure 6.6 Evaluation Rubric
Evaluating Compare and Contrast

WRITER _____ EVALUATOR _____

Circle one comment and corresponding number in each row that best tells how you respond to that trait of writing in a peer's draft. Multiply the circled number by the points listed at the end of the row, and place the product in the margin at the right. Total the numbers in the right-hand margin as a raw score and convert it, using page 142. Change any comments to represent your evaluation more accurately.

Voice (Vocabulary)

1	2	3	4	5	× 3 pts =
You seem to use only words that you can spell.		Good. You spell some vivid words the best that you can.		Your words show clear details about your ideas.	

Beginning

1	2	3	4	5	× 4 pts =
Your writing starts without telling about some basic features of objects in your mind.		You mention some important details from the start. Add even more.		Your beginning words start painting a picture of the objects in my mind.	

Common Features of the Objects

1	2	3	4	5	× 4 pts =
Your words do not tell me what the objects look like at all.		Your words tell me about some common features. There is need for more.		Your words help me visualize the objects in my mind.	

Differences Between the Objects

1	2	3	4	5	× 3 pts =
Your words do not tell me the differences at all.		Your words tell me some differences. Show me more.		Your words show me the differences between the objects.	

Ending

1	2	3	4	5	× 3 pts =
Your draft stops before I see the objects at all.		Your draft stops before I see the objects fully.		Your ending gives me full and final details.	

Proofreading

1	2	3	4	5	× 3 pts =
Errors prevent me from understanding your meaning		Errors interrupt the flow of meaning in your first draft.		I had to look hard to find any errors in your draft.	

Translated Score: _____   **Total Raw Score:** _____

Following a full response to rigorous topic prompts, students feel prepared to accept an invitation to prewrite with you. Chapter 7 demonstrates how to invite students to prewrite with you in a way that develops a mindset for revision. Chapter 8 presents a powerful way to add rigor to students' first drafts. Chapters 9 through 11 present a variety of ways to prompt students to return to their first drafts and revise them significantly. Chapters 12 and 13 present tools for preparing and presenting final drafts. Once students have worked through the writing process with the rigor of *Writer's Workshop for the Common Core*, they realize that making choices is an essential part of each step of the writing process.

Looking Back

In your response journal, describe two ideas about My Assignment Page as a tool for analyzing a writing topic prompt that you found valuable to you as a teacher in courses that you presently teach.

Looking Ahead

What things coming up in your curriculum invite you to adopt or adapt My Assignment Page with your students?

Chapter 7

Prewrite with Me

> **Common Core State Standards for Writing**
>
> Text Types and Purposes—2. Write informative/explanatory texts to examine and convey complex ideas and information clearly and accurately through the effective selection, organization and analysis of content.
>
> Production and Distribution of Writing—4. Develop and strengthen writing as needed by planning, revising, editing, rewriting or trying a new approach.
>
> **Common Core State Standards for Language**
>
> Vocabulary Acquisition and Use—4. Determine or clarify the meaning of unknown and multiple-meaning words and phrases based on grade-appropriate reading and content, choosing flexibly from a range of strategies.
>
> Vocabulary—5. Demonstrate understanding of figurative language, word relationships and nuances in word meanings.

"Take the first step in faith. You don't have to see the whole staircase, just take the first step."

—Martin Luther King, Jr.

Once students understand a topic fully, invite them to prewrite, to complete the task on which all later writing tasks depend. If you are thinking, What does prewriting have to do with revision or proofreading or publishing?—I know how you feel. I felt the same way for years before I found out that prewriting has everything to do with all that follows. Prewriting is like human feet, or so podiatrists claim. These medical practitioners hold that when we correct problems in our feet, the health of the rest of the body increases significantly. When foot problems go unaddressed, health issues throughout the rest of the body go unexplained. Then, of course, prewriting is like the human spine, say chiropractors. They claim that a well-aligned spine is the key to a healthy lifestyle. You need not buy into these philosophies, but in the study of human behavior, scientists agree that there are root causes of life's successes and problems. Similarly, problems later in the writing process can often be traced back to inadequate prewriting. The degree to which students succeed in prewriting determines the quality of their first and final drafts.

In a Writing Cycle, prewriting appears as the word bank (Figure 7.1). It follows on the heels of My Assignment Page on Monday and Tuesday and sets students up for drafting on Wednesday in the weekly plan for writing a first draft.

The word bank instills in students a sense of confidence for producing authentic writing. The three essential strategies of word banks include brainstorming, jot listing and arranging.

- **Brainstorming** requires students to think of more than one way to respond to a writing topic prompt before they choose one on which to write. This is a new way of prewriting for most students. The word bank requires students to brainstorm six possible responses to a writing topic

Figure 7.1   Word Bank: 1st Draft #1 of a Writing Cycle Based on a Genre

Mini-lesson—**M L** (7–10 min); work time—**W** (15–20 min); close—**C** (7–10 min)

Day →		Monday	Tuesday
Working Portfolio: 1st Draft # 1	M L	Invite and Model My Assignment Page and **word bank.**	Small-group conference **Word Study strategy for others : analogies.**
	W	Do My Assignment Page (5 min whole group). Look and Learn Two students share. Do the word bank (15 min). ***Brainstorm possible topics.** ***Jot list one topic.** **Teacher identifies students with incomplete word banks for a small-group conference on Tuesday.**	Do Word Study (PALS). **Three analogies based on each: science, math and/or social studies.**
	C	**Author's chair close (7–10 min).** Look and Learn **Students share their written efforts with PALs or in small groups or a whole group to receive coaching. Listening students mention two strengths and one question about the author's writing.**	

prompt. They quickly learn the benefits of brainstorming once they've chosen a response that was the third or fourth in their brainstorm list.

- **Jot listing** helps students deposit vivid words in word banks that describe the pictures in their minds about their topics.
- **Arranging** the words from brainstorming and jot listing helps students create a plan for writing their first drafts.

So how do you get students who don't like to write all that much to give prewriting a try? Easy. Ask a student to read the statement in the gray bar at the bottom of the word bank.

> For the word bank, earn 30 points by completing every line on this page. Use only vivid words and phrases—no sentences.

This statement quantifies expectations, gives the students credit for reaching those expectations and requires them to self-assess their performance before they move on. The stakes are higher for the word bank; this page is not a 20-pointer like My Assignment Page; it's worth a full 30 points or roughly one-third of the grade of their first draft. Most students get busy filling up the lines on this page with vivid words and no sentences, just like the gray bar states. When you see that there are students who need extra help, place them in PALS or group conference with them on the following day.

Mini-Lesson with Scripting for a Word Bank

INVITE

Brainstorm possible responses to the topic, then choose one. Jot list vivid details and arrange them for a first draft.

Teacher: **Prewrite with me.** Once I understand a writing topic prompt, one of two things happens. Sometimes I get excited about the topic and want to get busy writing. Other times, I read the topic and think, How am I going to get started? Either way, I've discovered that I need a word bank, so I invite you to prewrite with me using a word bank. A completed word bank sets your writing in motion and helps you write a first draft that others will want to read.

A word bank includes three important parts. The first is **brainstorming.** We'll brainstorm together first, and you'll see that it is important to think of five or six different ways that you could write about the writing topic prompt. The second part is **jot list(s).** This first time we'll jot list together so you'll have strong, vivid words to use in your first draft. The third is **arranging,** and I'll show you how to make a plan by yourself for using these strong words. It's that simple, and you'll be ready to write for your audience. Khalil's model word bank (page 56) shows you how.

MODEL

Review a completed word bank on a previous topic.

After a model experience with a group-created word bank, students readily prewrite on a second word bank with a PAL or on their own. Again, your role shifts from guide to facilitator/monitor. You make sure that students fill in the blanks with vivid and informative words and phrases. As students fill out word banks on their own, review their work and help students strengthen their word choice as needed.

Look at Khalil's word bank (Figure 7.2, page 56) and share his model with your students. He was one of twenty-five Rainbow Elementary School students at risk for not meeting the standard of his state's Grade 5 Writing Assessment. Like others in the group, he had successfully dodged prewriting until I introduced him to the word bank. This model was his third experience with a Word Bank for Compare and Contrast, and the first one completed on his own. His confident prewriting is obvious. At his teacher's suggestion, he brainstormed three holidays that he liked best and least—circling Christmas as best and St. Patrick's Day as least. St. Patrick's Day made the class curious. Why didn't he like a holiday that so many people are eager to celebrate?

Note that he circled the two holidays he could write the most about and drew an arrow to Differences—A and Differences—B. This simple graphic helps students keep their thoughts clear as they compare and contrast two holidays. It worked for Khalil. Before he deposited vivid words and phrases about the two holidays in his bank, his teacher led the whole class in jot listing common features of most holidays in their experience.

Khalil was ready to roll, and roll he did. In a matter of minutes, he filled up his first and third jot lists, ending with a flourish that left "30 points" in large, dark lead at the top of the page. His word bank was full, and he was ready to arrange the words from his brainstorm and jot list for writing his first draft.

He followed this procedure from the mini-lesson using a word bank.

- Write a phrase that describes the writing topic prompt at the top of the word bank. Khalil wrote, "My best and worst holidays." The phrase reminded Khalil to use words from the writing topic prompt in his first paragraph.
- Draw a circle of the title of the topic prompt at the top of the word bank large enough to include the entire brainstorm list, but not the

Figure 7.2 Khalil's Word Bank

30 points   PREWRITING

My Best and Worst Holidays

Word Bank for Compare and Contrast

BRAINSTORM: Your class or your teacher will help you list several pairs
of items to contrast or compare. Circle the pair from the list that you   #1
picture most clearly in your mind. Limit yourself to the kind of pairs your
teacher prompts (animals, people, places, objects, events or ideas).

Like Best		Like Least
1. New Year's	4.	Valentine's Day
2. (Christmas)	5.	Thanksgiving
3. Fourth of July	6.	(St. Patrick's Day)

Jot Lists: In the columns, list the phrases that you can use to contrast or
compare your two items. Choose the words that will help the readers of your
paper picture the items in their minds.

A—Differences	Common Features	B—Differences	
Mashed potatoes, ham, turkey, pies, tea, beans, cranberry sauce	←food →	Grits and eggs, mac and cheese	#2
Wii, rollerblades, guitar	←gifts →	None	#3
Family reunion	←get together →	Just school, nothing special	
Open gifts, pray, church program	←celebration →	When you pinch someone	#4
Pin the tail on the donkey, treasure hunt	←activities →	Pinching, joking, laughing, pointing	
New clothes, dress up	←attire →	Something green and easy to see	

Circle three common features with their A and B differences that you picture
the best in your mind. Write a full paragraph about each of these features, about
how the two items are alike (compare) and different (contrast).

For the word bank, earn 30 points by completing every line on this page.
Use only vivid words and phrases—no sentences.

jot lists. Place a *1* next to this large circle; these are the details for your first paragraph.

- Follow the directions at the bottom of the page just above the gray bar: Circle three common features with the A and B differences that you picture the best in your mind. Write a full paragraph about each of these features, noting how the two items are alike (compare) and different (contrast). Notice how Khalil placed a *2, 3* and *4* by these circles in the order that he chose to present them. A good rule of thumb for young writers: place #4 by the circle that you picture the best in your minds.

Caution: Prewriting that gives a false sense of achievement

Scaffold versus formula. A word bank provides a scaffold that leads students through strong, independent choices as they organize their thoughts. A formula overpowers authentic thought, producing contrived writing. Khalil's word bank helped him package his writing in four organized parts, but it did not restrict him to four paragraphs, nor did it tell him what to put in each paragraph. Rather, it empowered him to order them based on the mental pictures he wanted the words to deliver to his grandmother, with the strongest picture last. As he involved himself in drafting, he wrote two paragraphs about one part and an additional paragraph in a short conclusion. On the other hand, formula writing teaches students to create precisely five paragraphs: an introductory paragraph, three body paragraphs and a concluding paragraph. The formula tells students what kind of sentences to put in each paragraph (a topic sentence, three detail sentences and a clincher sentence). It leads them to believe that they are finished only when they have written five paragraphs even if

- They have only two supporting ideas. They resort to making a third body paragraph or repeating one already presented. The formula doesn't permit variation.
- They have more than three supporting ideas to include. They leave one out, sometimes the most important one.

Khalil avoided lapsing into formula writing in his plans for his introductory paragraph. He introduced his draft by describing what he was thinking when he first read the writing topic prompt. By contrast, formula writing dictates that the first sentence of the introductory paragraph hook the readers' attention in one of several ways introduced in a writing lesson. It continues by requiring the writer to introduce the topic sentence of each of the three body paragraphs and then to wrap up the introduction with what some formula writing programs call a thesis statement.

Prewriters following a formula run into problems because they have been taught to follow the formula regardless of their own thoughts. They feel locked into making their thoughts fit the formula. Read fifth-grader Gary's five-paragraph formula.

Title	Why I need my own cell phone.
Introduction	I will tell you three reasons why I need my own personal cell phone.
#1	The first reason I need a cell phone is because all my friends have them.
#2	The second reason I need a cell phones is because of an emergency.
#3	The third reason I need a cell phone is because I won't stop begging until you buy me one.
Conclusion	In conclusion, you see that I gave you three reasons why I need a cell phone now!

End of formula, end of writing. Interestingly, Gary reported that he added the third reason as he wrote because the formula required it. And the conclusion implies that because the writer created three reasons, his writing should be convincing. Nothing could be further from the truth. Instead of delivering the energy and power that Gary's argument needs, the formula drains the power out of Gary's ideas at each stage of the formula. Too bad; however, Gary's story has a good ending: he is now in a middle school that provides Writing Cycle packets for all students. His authentic voice, pictures and flow have already begun to blossom with just enough structure to serve as scaffolding, but not too much to stifle authentic thought.

Prewriting in Other Grades and Content Areas

> **MODEL**
>
> *Review a completed word bank on a previous topic.*

Khalil and his fifth-grade peers soared with the support of word banks, but how about third-graders? Certainly they require a different instructional tool; one size cannot possibly fit all. Actually, in the case of the word bank, one size does. Consider Ms. Beasley's third-graders at Ringgold Elementary School in their Writing Cycle for expository genre. They met three Explain a Process Word Banks: one based on personal experience, one based on an art project and one based on a science lesson. There were differences between how third- and fifth-graders approached word banks.

- The third-graders were more eager to fill up the word banks before they understood the specific expectations.
- They also needed the help of others in creating jot lists that contained truly vivid words—words that painted pictures in the minds of any reader.

- They prewrote the first word bank for a mode of writing as a whole group just like fifth-graders, but they needed the support of a small group or their PALs when they used the same word bank on later writing topics.
- A few third-graders peeled away from group prewriting in the course of the year, but not many (usually five to ten students out of a class of twenty-five). By contrast, all but four fifth-graders in a class of twenty-five prewrote independently in their second experience with a specific word bank.

Figure 7.3 on page 60 shows a Word Bank for Explain a Process.

Note: An example of the word banks that teachers find useful to have at their fingertips appears in "Prewriting," *The Writing Cycle for Writer's Workshop*. Athens, GA: Erincort Consulting, 2011. Character Sketch, Compare and Contrast, Description (place), Description (object), Explain a Cause, Explain a Solution, Explain an Effect, Explain a Problem, Explain a Process, Imaginative Writing, Interpretation, Narration, Personal Letter, Poetry: Free Verse, A Story-Making Kit, Summarizing: Researching, Support an Opinion and Support a Solution.

Prewriting for Voice, Pictures and Flow

> **LOOK**
>
> Peer-assess the brainstorm, jot list, and arrangement of your PAL's word bank.

Writing topic prompts force students to point their thoughts to the state standard, but they must stay in their minds with their thoughts as they do. A big part of the success of the word bank as a prewriting tool will be your use of the terms *voice*, *pictures* and *flow*. By contrast, both under-directed quick-writes and over-directed formulas for prewriting fall short in moving students to standards of authentic writing. Neither approach ensures that students' ideas become pictures for the readers to access, that their style emerges from the writing with a clear voice or that the organization ensures a seamless flow.

So ask your students to PAL up and identify the evidence of voice, pictures and flow in the prewriting plan of each other's word bank. Evidence of voice and pictures will appear in the vivid words of their jot lists; evidence of flow will appear in the circled sections of their word bank that sketched the plan for organizing their first drafts. When PALs have finished responding, let one or two PALs report what they have done.

In a professional development session, a group of teachers new to using the word bank for prewriting mentioned these elements and benefits for their teaching practices and in the learning habits of their students:

Figure 7.3 Word Bank for Explain a Process

30 points   A GAME I CAN TEACH YOU TO PLAY

> Prompt: Think about a game you enjoy. You have a friend who has never
> played the game but wants to learn. In a report to your friend, describe
> the game and explain how it is played. Be sure to explain the rules, the
> equipment, the number of players and anything else your friend might need
> to know to play the game.

#1

Brainstorm: Your class or your teacher will help you list several processes that
you could write about. Circle the one that you picture most clearly in your mind.

1. Godzilla Unleashed   4. LIFE Pirates of the Caribbean
2. Monopoly   5. H-O-R-S-E
3. Blindman's Bluff   6. Chess

Jot List: Make sure that the process you circled is the one that you could write
the most about. Then in the column, list phrases for each step of that process.
Include people, places, locations and happenings without worrying about the
order just yet.

Details from the steps of the process that I picture in my mind	Numbered in the order they occur	
Organize the cards and the money.	2	
Open the board and put the game pieces on the letters.	1	#2
Read the instructions and start with the spinner.	3	
Watch out for Calypso and Raid squares	5	
Start at Caribbean or Singapore	4	#3
Have the most money after 45 minutes.	6	

Circle the first step of the process that you picture in your mind. Start
your first draft with it. Include all of the details for each step. Use all the
words that come to mind, not just the ones that you can spell.

> For the word bank, earn 30 points by completing every line on this page.
> Use only vivid words and phrases—no sentences.

Elements

- Brainstorm and jot list shows what is similar about all writing.
- A different jot list is needed for each mode of writing (character sketch, narration and such).
- Word banks include a simple way to arrange ideas for drafting.
- The bar at bottom quantifies expectations before students have time to ask.
- Word banks provide a place for students to self-assess and for teachers' approval or adjustment.

Benefits

- Provides a specific direction for starting a first draft that can apply to any topic.
- Helps students focus on what they are thinking.
- Gives confidence to those students who lack it.
- Provides needed structure.
- Stimulates authentic thought for all levels of students.
- Applies a scaffolding activity to all modes and genres of writing.
- Gives students the freedom to use the scaffold but does not require them to stick to it rigidly.
- Helps students who have too many thoughts to control.
- Requires students with few thoughts to come up with additional ideas and details.
- Appears very structured, but produces authentic writing.
- Provides an alternative to students who use patterned introductions like, "In this paper I'm going to. . . ."

By contrast, third-graders explained their take on using the Explain a Process Word Bank for prewriting after three word bank experiences.

Elements

"We get to brainstorm and jot list on every word bank."
"The gray bar tells us how to make points."
"There is a place at the top to write my points."

Benefits

"It is fun and easy."
"It gives me a lot to write about."
"It makes me want to write."

"It's a bank to withdraw words from [echoing a teacher]."
"People help us write picture words in it."
"It gives us points for filling up the lines."
"It helps me write a two-pager."

Tips for Using Word Banks

Keep using word banks until students brainstorm and jot list fully without them. Just like training wheels on a bicycle, students need them until they write with balance and confidence, launching each multi-paragraph writing with substantial thought. Some principles of learning just don't change.

Stop using word banks at the earliest evidence of automaticity. When students fill them with vivid details like an order pad at a short-order restaurant, switch them to lined paper on which they write the headings "Brainstorm" and "Jot List," labeling each jot list when their writing calls for more than one.

Continue to prewrite with your students, storing your own word banks on your computer to be used later and shared with students and colleagues. Time students' prewriting until you see that all students get down to productive brainstorming and jot listing without the help of a timer. Close each prewriting day by letting students share in PALS or small groups. Most importantly, when students complete a word bank, they feel (and state) that they are

- Pleased with the pictures of their thoughts in their minds
- Proud of, even excited about, the plan they have created
- Ready to write a first draft
- Eager to start writing

Note that a first draft follows immediately upon the heels of prewriting after you and your students have completed this step in your Working Portfolios. Teach to the standards of a writing genre in the Working Portfolios (prompt prewriting and drafting on separate days); test students' use of writing according to standards in the Unassisted Writing Sample (chapter 13).

Looking Back

In your response journal, describe two ideas about the word bank that were valuable for you as a teacher in courses that you presently teach.

Looking Ahead

What things coming up in your curriculum invite you to adopt or adapt the word bank that you have met in this chapter?

Chapter 8

Write First Drafts with Me

Common Core State Standards for Writing

Text Types and Purposes—2. Write informative/explanatory texts to examine and convey complex ideas and information clearly and accurately through the effective selection, organization and analysis of content.

Text Types and Purposes—3. Write narratives to develop real or imagined experiences or events using effective technique, well-chosen details, and well-structured event sequences.

Production and Distribution of Writing—5. Develop and strengthen writing as needed by . . . trying a new approach.

"Make a movie behind your eyelids."

—Nancie Atwell

After arranging the best words in their word banks, students are geared up to write. Until they are adept at drafting from their word banks, prompt them with three practical suggestions:

- Point to circle #1 on your word bank and close your eyes to see the picture in your mind when you brainstormed possible topics.
- Each circle on your word bank represents a picture in your mind and deserves a paragraph in your first draft. Mark off the first seven to ten lines on your paper to write out the words that describe the picture in your mind for circle #1. Spell the best you can; we'll fix misspellings later.

Note: Some teachers advise students to skip the introductory paragraph in first drafts. Mature writers have a better idea of what they are introducing after they have written the draft. Beginning writers benefit from directly stating their focus in an introductory paragraph as a light to guide their draft. The first introduction is often not all that great, but it provides a foundation for one that is (chapter 10).

- Write out all of the words that come to mind about the other circles in your word bank.

Khalil wrote his first draft (Figure 8.2, page 65). See his complete Working Portfolio, pages 7–8, at www.writingtowin.com). His word bank (page 56) provides clear direction for his first draft.

Let me guess. Some of your students still serve up short paragraphs with vague word choices even more so than Khalil. In that case, consider the Framed Draft strategy, which lets students experience the thrill of producing vivid language in multi-paragraph first drafts. For productive first experiences with a Framed Draft, post two charts of words on your wall to reduce the use of vague words and promote the use of vivid ones. Present a chart of "picture killers" (Figure 8.1) with a flourish to emphasize its importance.

Why not arrange a funeral service in which your students bury all of the words, never to use them again in this class? That is the intent. With this drama, students used far fewer picture killers in their writing than before. Direct PALs to coach each other in replacing these words at the close of a work session for writing a first draft.

Figure 8.1 Picture Killers

Outlawed Words (except in dialogue of characters)		
stuff	a lot	go (went)
truly	sort of	get
really	fine	said
very	weird	eat (ate)
awesome	fine	super
cool	thing	well
great	neat	you know
big	cute	_____
good	nice	_____
bad	guy	_____
nice	person	_____
kind of	dude	_____

Post a chart of "picture makers"—prepositions and conjunctions—without calling them by name (Figure 8.3, page 66). Call them function words. They enable students to deepen the descriptive powers of their words. The two charts speak clearly: use fewer adjectives and adverbs for

Figue 8.2 Khalil's First Draft

50 Points

Dear Grandma,

Thanks for inviting me out to your house for St. Pat's Day. I would like to come, but you see, there are holidays I like and there are some I don't. New Year's Christmas and 4th of July is my favorite. St. Pat's, Valentine's and Labor Day is my least. Thanks for the invitation, but I have to visit another time.

First, I don't like green much. You are supposed to have something green on your clothes that is easy to see but not everybody likes to wear green. When you show up at school, everywhere you look there is green except for the kids who forgot the day.

Here's another part about St. Pat's I don't like. If you don't wear green on St. Pat's you get pinched. I don't mean a playful little pinch. Some of the pinches could cause violence. Besides St. Pat's Day is ordinary. It is absolutely ordinary. St. Pat's is like a regular day. Absolutely regular. Days like Christmas and Thanksgiving and Easter, people mark on their calendars and wait for them to come. Nobody thinks about St. Pat's day before it comes.

Another thing about St. Pat's Day you don't get gifts. On another holiday such as Christmas you get gifts. What's a holiday without gifts? On Christmas I got a Wii, a Guitar and rollerblades. On St. Pat's I get nothing but pinched. On St. Pat's you eat green eggs and grits. Who wants that for breakfast? Yuck! On Christmas you eat hot and delicious food. On St. Pat's Day you eat green salad, green grits and green eggs and mac & cheese. On Christmas you eat turkey, potato salad and greens. Sorry grandma, but that is it. I can't come out on St. Pat's Day.

> For 1st Draft #3, earn 50 points for exceeding teacher expectations, 40 points for meeting teacher expectations and 0 to 30 points for missing teacher expectations.

creating written pictures. Create your ideas with phrases and clauses that develop richer and more powerful and graphic descriptions. The strongest part of the message is that your students need practice using descriptive phrases and clauses, not talking *about* them. Just let the charts prompt them to stop using picture killers and start inserting picture makers. Once they use them with ease, talk about prepositions and conjunctions in the patterns that they have learned *how* to use so well.

Figure 8.3 Picture Makers

Add vivid details with . . .		
above	over	toward
in	behind	under
on	at	with
for	under	up
of	before	until
when	who	through
that	about	_____
from	by	_____
to	during	_____
since	like	_____
between	near	_____
after	off	_____
as	through	_____

These charts are perfect to use for expanding the Framed Drafts presented in this chapter. They are also useful in revising the first drafts the students choose. Concrete, know-how revision strategies abound. For now, however, let's examine this Framed Draft that will launch your students on a productive journey of learning *how* to write so they can talk *about* what they have learned more comfortably.

Framed Drafts

Framed Drafts help students create first drafts with a sharpening eye for vivid detail about new knowledge they have met in their curriculum. The introductory Framed Draft (Figure 8.4, page 68) fits students studying biomes and aboriginal African cultures in social studies. You may want to create a Framed Draft based on text from curricula your students are studying instead of using the model of *Jungle Story* here.

Framed Drafts require students to insert multiple words into blanks within sentences. This process imprints in your students' minds the idea that, like Framed Drafts, their first drafts are incomplete for readers. It is normal for writers to return to their drafts and flesh out more details in order for readers to understand their ideas as well as they do. Although Framed Drafts exist apart from authentic student writing, the practice of completing Framed Drafts carries over to their independent writing (*Individualized Language Arts,* Weekawken, NJ: 1970).

Framed Drafts also provide the perfect opportunity for students to learn to operate outside of the casual or intimate language register that they use with their families and friends. Framed Drafts prompt students to add the details used in the more formal language of acquaintances or people whom they have just met. For some of your students, their writing from Framed Drafts will be the most vivid writing that they have created to date.

Framed Drafts further provide the general framework of paragraphs: varied sentence patterns with punctuation and structured paragraphs. All that is left for students to do is provide the additional specific, multiple-word details to expand the frame.

Lesson with Scripting for Framed Drafts

> **INVITE**
>
> *Use the plan in your word bank to complete a Framed Draft.*

Teacher: Write vivid Framed Drafts with me. Let's try something different today—a way to write that begins in a curious way. We'll create a first draft from a Framed Draft. All you need to do is sit back, relax and review our study of jungle life in a way that you've never done before; just give the writing task your best try. I know you will enjoy it!

This introductory Framed Draft (Figure 8.4) prompts you to write as many details as possible that come to your mind and fit them into the frame. As you add words, clear pictures of your thoughts begin to develop. Your fictional narrative must be realistic fiction, fiction that could actually occur using the langauge of the standard of our study of life in a rain forest biome. By consensus, the class will recognize the boy and the girl who add the most words that fit the frame and make an engaging narrative. They will present their drafts to an audience outside of the class.

Figure 8.4 Introductory Framed Draft

"The Jungle Story"

Possible Characters
scientist
photographer
lion
missionary
hunter
native
map maker
explorer
archaeologist
tourist

Function Words
in
on
over
but
for
who
that
which
because
against
although
of
from
at

One day _____ to the jungle. _____

wanted to find _____ for _____. All of

_____ came running to _____. They

were _____.

   The chief_____ was standing _____.

She was _____. She knew _____ and

decided to _____. She was _____.

   At last the _____ developed a

_____. With _____ they _____.

As they winged their way _____, they said,

"_____." _____ was very

_____.

Teacher: First I'll read all three paragraphs of the narrative. Follow along and let me know what you think of their potential.

> One day (blank) to the jungle. (Blank) wanted to find (blank) for (blank). All of the (blank) came running to . . . [and with a dramatic slowing down].
> . . . As they winged their way (blank), they said "(blank)." (Blank) was very (blank).

There you have it. It's a real narrative, right? What did you think of it? You're right, it *was* rather (blank). But what do you know for sure from the frame?

One class I met recently concluded the following:

Students: The setting is in a jungle.
A group visited the jungle with a specific purpose.
A crowd and a chief observed the arrival of visitors.

Teacher: So does it sound like you could improve on this narrative? Good. Let's get off to a solid start. First we brainstorm possible main characters as illustrated in the left margin of the model. Then we jot list small function words that will help us reach the minimum of five words per blank in the frame. See the list in the right margin of this introductory Framed Draft or the Picture Makers chart.

Take two minutes to add at least five more possible characters to the jot list in the left margin.

[After two minutes] I need to see you circle one or two of the characters that you will use in your personal Framed Draft.

Good. I see we all have one or two characters circled—and an interesting combination of characters there are!

Let's kick-start this task as a whole group. Who will provide us with four or five words that fit into the first blank, using your characters?

A student:	One day <u>a photographer and I went to</u> the jungle.
Teacher:	That is five words; it meets the minimum, but it contains a picture killer. Someone replace the offending word.
A student:	"took a plane" for "went"
Teacher:	Look at the function words in the left margin and insert words that make a better picture come to our minds.
A student:	<u>a photographer from the *Star-Tribune* in downtown Minneapolis and I boarded a Delta plane and flew to</u>

The point was made: seventeen words was not too many words to add. In fact, these seventeen words created an engaging first sentence. Why would a photographer from a big newspaper go with him to the jungle? I encouraged the same student to add five or more words in the second blank, and he offered, "<u>For ten years this boy and this man</u> wanted to find <u>a secret, healing waterfall in the mountains to photograph</u> for <u>their family and friends back home in Delano</u>." I had to stop this eager writer so he could commit his thoughts to paper and let the others launch their own thoughts.

<table>
<tr><td>

MODEL

Review a completed Framed Draft of a student/ teacher on a previous topic.

</td><td>

My model retained good evidence of the frame even though my first characters were natives of the jungle. I didn't think of a trip over to the jungle at all. I underlined the words that I added to each blank and circled the function word from the Picture Makers chart that I used on page 66.

</td></tr>
</table>

One day <u>a band of young aborigines in war dress left the Savannah and headed for the depths of</u> the jungle.

<u>Ever since explorers from a strange land drove them</u>

out of their thatched-hut village, they wanted to find a way to recapture their tribal plot for preparations for their annual celebration of the harvest. All of the fiercely painted young warriors came running through the familiar pathways without making a sound to catch the uninvited settlers by surprise. They were intent on their mission and would not be denied.

The chief warrior led the charge and in no time was standing on a bluff overlooking the plot of land the young men used to call home. He was satisfied that he had conditioned his troops sufficiently for the task. He knew them all by name and family background and decided to sound the alarm for surprise attack. He was certain it was the right time to ensure success.

At last the settlers from a strange land developed a sense that all was not well.

I did the math, too. As far as I wrote (34 words of the frame), I added 147 words in 15 blanks, or 9.8 words per blank. My model Framed Draft carried the desired effect. The students responded openly.

"You added so many words."
"The sentences didn't sound like run-ons."
"Can we add nine words to a blank if we want?"

Of course they could, and several of them did just that. But go ahead and write a model yourself.

Teacher: You have seven minutes to fill in the blanks of the Framed Draft with words that describe all of the pictures that start developing in your minds. Final tips:
1. If you think of words to add outside of the blanks, use them.
2. You can add more than one sentence to a blank.
3. Try to stick with the frame. If your narrative takes a different direction than the frame, I still expect the high level of details that you achieved in your additions to the blanks.

The introductory Framed Draft became quite entertaining, even though it was curriculum based. Yet the Framed Draft strategy has far more promise than fun in school. Look at the Framed Draft that Ms. Knight wrote to model Framed Drafts for her fifth-graders. It models the mode of writing called Explain a Classification (*A Writing Cycle for Writer's Workshop,* grades 3–8, p. D-12) and requires the students to recall their studies of urban life in the United States.

Where People Work

When people go to work, they do not all get dressed up in suits and ties. In fact, even workers who work at local elementary schools will wear blue jeans on dress-down days. There are as many different forms of clothing to wear on a job as there are jobs that people work hard at every day. And the products that the employees produce provide useful and necessary goods for consumers to enjoy.

Some places of work make products like delicious, hot, chocolate-glazed doughnuts. Huge buildings are necessary to produce these tasty confections, and many workers are responsible for completing the tasty treats. These factories contain assembly lines that allow these delicious confections to be transported through every step of the process, from the batter to the box. Workers are required to wear hairnets and gloves to keep the product pure. They make sure the product is perfect for the consumer.

Other stores, such as Food Lion, do not make products; they sell them. The buildings simply have shelves and cash registers, and people work there to keep the shelves stocked and check people out after they select the items they wish to buy. These stores can be large and locally owned or chain stores, or the retail location may be a small service station where you pick up a sleeve of powdered treats while buying gas. Buying and selling are important responsibilities for all markets.

Still other types of retail industries provide a service. The stores at Hamilton Place Mall provide many different services. The Wolf

Camera stores provide services such as printing photos, providing information about various cameras and supplying products to keep a camera safe. Having people work in different jobs helps others earn income so that they can provide for their families. New services keep being discovered that will allow Americans to continue earning wages.

Figure 8.5 Self-Assessment Math

Number of sentences in first draft	19 sentences
Teacher expectation, average words/sentence	2 or 3 words
Number of red words added	237 words
Average words/sentence added	12.5 words per sentence
Number of chart words added	38 (2 per sentence)
Self-assessment (circle one)	⊕ ◎ ▭

Note that her model demonstrates additions than her students could possibly achieve. When she read her model aloud, she moved through the response process she later expected of her students. She randomly identified three sentences and asked students

- If the additions fit each of the three sentences
- If she needed to add more, write less, or leave them as they were

DO
Write your Framed Draft on the current topic.

Her students were surprised that she added four times as many words as she expected of them. They were equally surprised that her sentences weren't too long to understand. Mary Margaret wrote a credible description of where Americans work. Here are her first two paragraphs.

Where People Work

When people go to work, they do not all do manual labor. In fact, even workers who work at landscaping companies will do paperwork of some sort. There are as many different types of work people do in one company as there are stars in the sky. And the landscaping companies also provide other services such as hedge sculpting, weed pulling and lawn mowing for their many customers.

   Some places of work make products like boxed chocolate. Huge buildings are full of dedicated workers and powerful machinery. These factories contain assembly lines so that the candy can ride down the conveyer belt and get put into boxes by the workers. This saves much time by shortening the process of making candy and keeping the workers moving fast. Workers box and handle the candy with a great deal of care. They make sure that all of the candy reaches the consumers without any damage whatsoever.

Mary Margaret did the math and looked up with a shocked smile on her face. She announced that she had never written a paper that was 288 words long before. Of course, 85 words were provided in the frame. She did add 191 in the 29 blanks, an average of 6.6 words per blank. A less practiced writer than Mary Margaret, Kayleigh discovered that her first expository framed draft let her write with voice and her additions showed that she trusted her thoughts.

   When people go to work, they do not all dress up in gressy shirts and sweaty hair neets. In fact, even workers who work at Unum Provident will dress up in nice clothes every day they are reguarded to wear less types of clothes. There are as many different jobs that you will dress in old jeans and t-shirts like there are in a food markets and gas station and the graden clubs where you will work in old jeans because you work in dirt. And the garden clubs provide people with nice gradens in there front yards and they can also grow fruits and vegetables for there gradens.

LOOK

Identify the voice, pictures, and/or flow in your PAL's Framed Draft.

   Actually, Mary Margaret and Kayleigh were PALs assigned to reflect on each other's first drafts. The routine included

- PAL A reading her first draft to PAL B verbatim
- PAL B identifying three sentences that made the clearest pictures come to her mind

- PAL A circling the three sentences that PAL B identified
- PAL B reading her framed draft for PAL A's response

Thanks to the work with two Framed Drafts in the expository genre, Ms. Knight reported the shortest learning curve for this genre among all levels of students. Unlike previous years, students' writing voices emerged in their expository writing as much as in their narrative writing.

> **LEARN**
>
> *Record the elements and benefits that your class creates of strong use of Framed Drafts.*

Student Self-Assessment: Students complete their Framed Drafts by assessing the degree to which they met your stated expectation. They need to add a minimum of five words per blank, and the additions need to paint clear pictures of their thoughts for the readers. When students add an average of five words per blank, they assess themselves a target ◉ (85 points). If they add fewer words per blank or their writing does not flow, they self-assess a bar ▱ (70 points). When they add more than five words, they self-assess a plus + (100 points).

A group of social studies students in a seventh-grade classroom shared these thoughts on the use of the framed draft:

> "You don't have to add five words to every blank. It's better if you don't."
> "You add a different number of words to each blank."
> "It was a little tough to add words to somebody else's sentences."
> "After about four blanks, I got the hang of it."
> "This was fun and easy."
> "I just add the details; the sentences were already there for me."
> "Adding ten or fifteen words to a blank wasn't too much."
> "Framed Drafts help us add really good details to my sentences."
> "We all started the same way, but our essays are way different."

Conclusion: Help students conclude that adding more details to a draft than usual makes writing that readers understand. They all need to realize that in writing a draft for an audience, they need to add many more words than they think they should, not fewer. Even students who exaggerated were surprised by how well their drafts read. Your students will definitely benefit from completing Framed Drafts. They may even find that a more elaborated style of writing fits them to a *T*.

Other Framed Drafts Based on a Social Studies Curriculum

View copies of the Framed Drafts in this chapter from www.writingtowin.com. Additional Framed Drafts in six modes of writing appear in *A Writing Cycle for Writer's Workshop* (pp. D-6–K-15). One is reprinted in Figure 8.6 below.

Figure 8.6 Character Sketch

The Trail Boss

Read through the following draft expressively, saying "blank" at every blank. Words that fit in the blanks will come to your mind as you read. You will see it is a frame for a first draft. On a clean sheet of lined paper, begin copying the frame up to the point of the first blank. Then add at least the minimum of seven words per blank. Use small function words such as *on, beside, that, at, from,* or *with* to help you reach the minimum. The more words you add, the more the frame will become your own, and the prouder you will be.

Trail bosses are usually found _____. They serve people who _____. Some bosses work _____ and _____. Trail rides often occur _____. The need for _____ bosses is growing _____.

In the saddle, trail bosses _____ and _____. They wear _____ and _____. They would never be seen _____ or _____. They may lead _____. With _____, they lead _____ with pride.

All trail bosses show _____ and _____ on the trail. In danger they _____. They also _____ people in good _____. They know when _____ and when _____. They even know _____ about _____. There is no _____ like a _____.

Final Thoughts on Writing First Drafts

Students bring greatly varied experiences to writing first drafts. Thankfully, Framed Drafts deliver benefits to the marginal and gifted alike. When students write first drafts freely from prewriting word banks, keep the following in mind:

- Students write a first draft only after the completion of an assignment page and word bank (or equivalent tools or strategies). I have not seen many tools of equivalent rigor or completeness; so many prewriting tools seem to be either too formulaic or not rigorous enough.
- Students keep their word banks in sight as they create their first drafts.
- Write along with students for 2 or 3 minutes before looking up to see if some are not writing. Approach a non-writing student only if your experience indicates that the student truly needs help.

- Students self-assess the moment they complete the task of drafting.
- Have word study and sentence study strategies, lessons and learning centers in place for students who finish ahead of others.
- Assign PALs an author's chair routine for the close of the work session, a concrete response strategy related to the writing task (see PALS appendix on page 189).

Looking Back

In your response journal, describe two ideas each about the Framed Draft that were valuable for you as a teacher in courses that you presently teach.

Looking Ahead

What things coming up in your curriculum invite you to adopt or adapt the Framed Drafts that you have met in this chapter?

Chapter 9

Revise Words and Phrases with Me

"It's better to work through the writing process fewer times thoroughly than to rush through the process frequently."

—Donald Murray

An Introduction to Revising First Drafts

Jot and Blend is a concrete, specific—and beneficial—revision strategy that all levels of students embrace eagerly. It is one of four revision strategies that you will take away from this book. Students can master the revision step of the writing process much more easily than my teacher colleagues and I previously thought. I hope you'll add these strategies to your writing toolkit. But first, the setup that allows these revision strategies to work their magic.

Your students have completed three first drafts on three separate topics in a writing genre that they have presented for specific responses to their PALs, a small group, or the whole class. To meet or exceed the standard of a writing genre, they need to revise only one of these three first drafts to take it through to publication. Let students pick the first draft that they like the best. What a refreshing contrast to the idea that revision is for writing that needs the most help! So then, effective revision includes

- Selecting a worthy first draft
- Rereading the first draft
- Following a concrete, easy-to-understand revision strategy to add, delete, move or rewrite ideas

Look in on Khalil after he selected 1st Draft #1 as his best first draft. His teacher, Ms. Benta, set an average of three words added per sentence as the expectation on the Writing Cycle Log for Teacher Expectations wall chart (page 79), using Jot and Blend. She chose Jot and Blend as she skimmed the students' selected first drafts and saw that all students' drafts needed details throughout.

In addition to Ms. Benta's description of a revision task on the wall chart, she personalized the task for each student with a First Draft Response Form (page 80) for each of her twenty-three students. Response forms include a primary-trait scoring rubric and a written teacher commentary. This rubric focuses on a primary trait of topic development, organization and detail. Introduce this page by letting a student read the information in the gray bar at the bottom of the page (see also page 17 of an exemplar Writing Portfolio at www.writingtowin.com).

> The number that your teacher circles indicates the grade your first draft will receive with no revisions: 1=F, 2=D, 3=C, 4=C, 5=B, 6=A.

Teachers circle a number between 1 and 4 on the rubric to give students the clear message that they need to revise. All first drafts need to go through one or more revision strategies. Students should never hear that their first draft is so well written that it does not need to be revised.

As you can see from Figure 9.2 on page 80, Ms. Benta circled a *4*, telling Khalil his writing approached, but did not meet, the standard (earning a C) if he left it as it was. In two sentences of the teacher commentary, she prompted him to meet or exceed standard.

Figure 9.1

Writing Cycle Log *for Teacher Expectations*
A Project of the Writing Process (completed by Ms. Benta)

Modes of Writing

A Narration	G Explain a problem	M Poetry
B Description	H Explain a process	N Summarizing
C Character sketch	I Explain a solution	O Support an opinion/
D Imaginative writing	J Interpretation	solution
E Explain a cause/effect	K Compare/contrast	P Miscellaneous
F Explain a classification	L Letter	

Step	Mode	**Teacher Expects	Description of Topic	Points
*1st Draft #1	K	4 ¶s	Favorite and least favorite holidays (Half of the points are from your prewriting and half from your first draft.)	85
*1st Draft #2	K	4 ¶s	Helping a friend choose between two pets for a gift	85
*1st Draft #3	C	4 ¶s	A person who has been influential to me	85
Revision	K	3 words/ sentence	Jot and Blend three words per sentence in one first draft. (A description of how I used this revision strategy in my first draft.)	85

* Includes a completed assignment page, word bank and first draft
**Description of what it takes to meet the standard ◎ and earn 85 points

Based on his final draft, Khalil takes Ms. Benta's two-sentence commentary to heart and adds in the detailed description of Christmas that did not appear in his first draft (see Khalil's final draft at www.writingtowin.com). Page 81 shows the Writing Cycle for Student Self-Check.

Focus the writing task for week 4 of a Writing Cycle on specific revision strategy like Jot and Blend and the creation of a final draft. As an example, launch the writing tasks for the week with Monday's mini-lesson.

- On the Friday before week 4, identify your first draft for me to review with the First-Draft Response Form (page 17 of your Working Portfolio).

Figure 9.2 First-Draft Response Form

Topic Development, Organization and Detail

Writer: Khalil Mehta

Evaluator: Ms. Benta

Title: Christmas and St. Pat's Day

➢ Little or no topic development, organization, or detail.	1
➢ Beginning of topic development visible, beginning of organizational plan visible.	2
➢ Clear topic, but development is incomplete, a clear plan with loosely organized ideas.	3
➢ Very clear topic, but complete development is uneven; beginning, middle and/or end may be clumsy.	(4)
➢ Fully developed topic. Clear beginning, middle and end. Organization sustains the writer's purpose.	5
➢ Fully elaborated topic. Organization sustains the writer's purpose and moves the reader.	6

Teacher commentary:

Khalil,

The contrast between Christmas and St. Pat's is becoming quite clear. Jot and blend more details about Christmas from your jot list in paragraphs 2, 3, 4 and 6.

PS: Good idea to use the letter format.

- Review my assessment of your first draft and my written commentary. It will tell you how to meet or exceed the standard in your final draft.
- Choose whether you want to meet or exceed my expectations for a specific revision strategy.
- Revise (pages 18–19 of your Working Portfolio).
- Complete the peer-revision rubric on your assigned PALs' revision (pages 18–19 of your Working Portfolio).
- Make additional changes to your draft based on your PALs' peer-revision response (bottom of page 19 of your Working Portfolio).
- Create a final draft that integrates your revisions into your final draft.
- Make additional revisions as you write.
- Share your final draft at author's chair with your small PALS group.

Figure 9.3

Name: Khalil Mehta
Beginning Date: October 12
End Date: December 4

Writing Cycle Log *for Student Self-Check*
A Project of the Writing Process

Modes of Writing		
A Narration	**F** Explain a classification	**L** Letter
B Description	**G** Explain a problem	**M** Poetry
C Character sketch	**H** Explain a process	**N** Summarizing
D Imaginative writing	**I** Explain a solution	**O** Support an opinion/
E Explain a cause/effect	**J** Interpretation	solution
	K Compare/contrast	**P** Miscellaneous

Step	Mode	**Self-Check	Description of Topic	Points
*1st Draft #1	K	+	Christmas and St. Pats Day (Half of the points are from my prewriting and half from my first draft.)	95
*1st Draft #2	K	+	Choose a cat or a snake.	90
*1st Draft #3	C	◎	My principal, Dr. Roberts	80
Revision	K	+	I needed to add three words per sentence. I added six words per sentence on average. (A description of how I used this revision strategy in my first draft.)	85

* Includes a completed assignment page, word bank and first draft
** **Key:** + exceeds expectations ◎ meets expectations ▭ misses expectations

Feel free to list these steps for pacing on your wall or provide copies for your students to check off as they complete them.

Figure 9.4 (page 83) shows how the pacing chart looks in chart form.

A Routine for Introducing Revision

Once you establish the need for each of your students to revise with a First Draft Response Form, your students are ready to stretch for the

Common Core State Standard for revision (and the next 100 points). Follow the same learning sequence that you used in prewriting: invite, model, do (revise), look (reflect) and learn (identify elements and benefits of the writing task). Begin by saying to students, I . . .

Invite   you to look at your first drafts with me and meet the revision strategy of the week: Jot and Blend.

Model   the strategy in adult writing to help you picture how Jot and Blend works.

Do   my own writing and want you to Jot and Blend the best you can on your writing also.

Look   with you at what each of us has revised.

Learn   with you how the revision strategy improved all of our first drafts.

To introduce revision, I use this script, which works with the least and most capable of writers:

Teacher: You have written three first drafts and selected one that you like the best. So tell me, who were you writing your first drafts for?

[Students normally respond, "You," or "our teacher."]

Teacher: Are you sure? I read over your first drafts. I think you wrote them for yourselves! You missed a good number of details. Trust me, you really want to do something to your first drafts before others read them. I know I want help with my first draft. You help me and I'll help you. Deal?

[Some students agree. Others think that their drafts are ready to hand in. The first time I revise with students, I begin with the following.]

Teacher: Anyone know what the word revision means?

[If I hear "correct mistakes," "fix my writing," or "do the paper over," I ask the question again.]

Teacher: Just a minute, now. Slow down. Look at the word *revision*, like in a dictionary. It seems to have two parts, right? What are the two? Who wants to take a stab at it?

[I instruct them to write *revision* at the top of their first draft and do the same myself on the board. A student comments, "the two parts are *re-* and *–vision*." I place a slash between the *e* and the *v*.]

Figure 9.4   Revision: A Writing Cycle for Writer's Workshop

Prime I (7–10 min), mini-lesson (**ML**); Prime III (15–20 min), workshop (**W**); Prime II (7–10 min), close (**C**)

Day →		Monday	Tuesday	Wednesday	Thursday	Friday
Revision of one first draft	**M L**	**Invite and Model** **Revision includes . . .** **Jot and Blend** revision strategy	**Word Study** or **Sentence Study:** vivid verbs	**Invite and Model** **for Peer-revisers** of first drafts	**Invite and Model** Model for creating a final draft with additional revision in the draft	**Invite and Model** Weekly **Author's Chair**
	W	**Do (write)** **Revise** one first draft with Jot and Blend • **Teacher IDs students** with incomplete revisions for small group work tomorrow.	**Do (write)** **Two groups** • **Teacher** coaches students with incomplete revision. • **Other students** use thesaurus to improve five to seven verbs in first drafts.	**Do (write)** **Peer Revision** • PALs complete revision rubric for each other's revision and follow their PAL's advice.	**Do (write)** **Create final draft** from first draft and revisions, making further revisions. • **Word study** or **sentence study** when final drafts are complete.	**Look (share and respond)** Whole group **Author's Chair** • Four or five students share revised drafts in small groups and ID voice, pictures and flow; one shares with the whole group.
	C	**Look (share and reflect)** **Author's Chair close** (5–7 min) • Students share their written task with their PALs to receive coaching following a specific response strategy.				**Learn (explain)** Whole group lists elements/ benefits of Jot and Blend.

Teacher: So, what do the two parts mean? Someone start with the first part.

[I hear, "*Re-* means 'over.'"]

Teacher: Exactly. *Re-* means again. It means you do something again. So tell me, what have you already done in your first draft that you can do over again? Did you correct errors in your first draft, so you can correct them again?

[Students reject this notion, but have little to offer in its place. Hearing no comments, I continue.]

Teacher: What's a vision? What does vision have to do with writing a first draft?

[Realization sinks in for a student or two. "Oh, yeah! Ms. Almond told us, You have a picture in your mind when you write your first draft." Several say the same thing in different ways. Then the class all speaks about their acquaintance with the terms *voice, pictures* and *flow.*]

Teacher: So, in revision, you picture again what you were thinking when you wrote your first draft? Why would you want to do that?

[A student understands and says, "You look back at the pictures in your head and see if your writing makes readers see the same pictures."]

Teacher: Then the first draft isn't for other people. If it isn't for other people, who is the first draft written for?

[Several students respond, "First drafts are written for us." Class consensus is achieved.]

Teacher: So does anyone still believe that first drafts are written for teachers?

[No answer.]

Teacher: Good. So you are the only ones who presently see the pictures beneath your first drafts. Now we can revise!

Truth #1 about Revision

Revision of first drafts is an inside-the-mind task.
Specific suggestions from readers (including teachers) do not lead to authentic revision. All effective revision strategies prompt students to revise their first drafts themselves. Effective student revisers
- **Brainstorm** possible revisions in a draft
- **Choose** the best one(s) for a specific draft

Authentic revision starts from the writer's thoughts. Only after students have tried a revision strategy do they benefit from the suggestions of their teachers or peers. When they get suggestions from others before they begin revising, students virtually turn their writing over to others. Actually, the best ideas for revision are inside their own heads.

Truth #2 about Revision

Concrete revision strategies that lead to authentic revision prompt students to make choices about revision that are easy to make and quick to show improvements. All choices and revisions work best when they are written in a contrasting color; I issue red pens for students to use and claim that there is magic in them. "When you read your first draft with a red pen in hand, extra words pop back into your mind. Red pens are the best tool for jotting down those words and blending them into your first drafts." When classes of students start adding red words and phrases to their sentences, they experience the satisfaction of seeing red on papers spread throughout the classroom. When students are jotting down red words with fluency, I'll quip, "My goodness, the red words are spreading all over this classroom."

Truth #3 about Revision

The choice of which revision strategy is best for each student's first draft comes after experience with concrete, intentional strategies like those in chapters 9 through 11. After practicing the following revision strategies with students, help them learn to identify which revision strategy best fits their first drafts. They are not listed in order of maturity, difficulty, or importance.

Level 1	Words and phrases	Jot and Blend (chapter 9)
Level 2	Sentences	Sentence Check Chart; combining sentences (chapter 11)
Level 3	Paragraphs	Circling picture sentences; writing leads; writing closes (chapter 10)

At first, students benefit from everyone working a revision strategy at the same time. Once students meet strategies at several levels, place them in small groups with others who will benefit from the same revision strategy. Start where I did several years ago: pick one strategy at a time and work it until you get it to produce impressive results in most students' writing. Try the others in the order that they appear in *Writer's Workshop for the Common Core*. In a year or two, you will develop comfort in helping students select the best revision strategies for their drafts with precision.

Revise Words and Phrases with Me

In prompting students to revise first drafts, invite them to jot down details—more than they need—in every sentence and return later to blend them into the words around them. Jot and Blend is the most accessible revision strategy to students and applies in some degree to every first draft written. This chapter presents two students whose first drafts benefitted from the Jot and Blend strategy. Feel free to use them as models for your students until you develop ones of your own.

Lesson with Scripting for Jot and Blend

INVITE
Revise your first draft usisng Jot and Blend.

Teacher: **Jot and blend details with me.** Our minds are remarkable organs. When we reread one of our first drafts, extra words and phrases pop into our minds. They were already there, but they haven't come out for us to use yet. That's why we all have red pens in hand. So read each sentence of your first draft one at a time. As the details occur to you, jot them down above the place they belong in each sentence. Don't worry about making all the details fit just yet; just jot them down. Use the words listed on the Picture Makers chart. Let your pen try to keep up with your mind. Jot down details whether they fit or not; blend in what you choose to use when you create your final draft.

MODEL
Review a revised first draft that used Jot and Blend on a previous topic.

Two students from other schools, who are just about your age, wrote first drafts similar to yours. Mackenzie and Ishmael presented their thoughts on topics about owls and the 2010 earthquake in Haiti after revising them with Jot and Blend (the picture makers are circled). Mackenzie, a third-grader in life science class at Ringgold Elementary School, wrote an expository draft of her research from the Internet on owls.

Outrageous Owls

Hey, did you know that owls are raptors? They are nocturnal raptors (because) they are asleep (in) the day and hunt at night. That's pretty outrageous, but not (as) outrageous (as) their heads. An owl can turn its head 3/4 of a circle. They even regurgitate pellets every day. That's the bones left (from) the prey that they eat. Owls are amazing creatures!

Owls have eyes that can see a whole room away. They have three . . .

Figure 9.5 Student Self-Assessment

Number of sentences in first draft	_____
Teacher expectation, average words per sentence	_____
Number of red words added	_____
Average words per sentence added	_____
Self-assessment (circle one)	+ ◎ ▭

Ishmael, a fifth grader from Canby Lane Elementary School, persuaded his classmates to choose a project for helping others that he liked the best.

I know (we) are all friends, (and) we all like the projects (that) we chose the best. Ms. Quillet says we can only pick one, and I think my project is the best one (for) our class (to) pick. We could clean up the school yard (but) that's the janitors jobe. We could pick up litter on Greenway Drive (but) neighbors should pick up there own trash (on) their own property. We could help kids in kindergarten learn to read (but) they already have two teachers (in) there rooms. I think the best project is to collect money for Haiti.

First, we can help Haiti by donating money (for) repairs. . . .

Figure 9.6 Student Self-Assessment

Number of sentences in first draft	_____
Teacher expectation, average words per sentence	_____
Number of red words added	_____
Average words per sentence added	_____
Self-assessment (circle one)	+ ◎ ▭

Once Mackenzie and Ishmael completed the Jot and Blend strategy, their teachers posted their final drafts on the classroom wall as exemplars for others to read and follow.

Prompting the Jot and Blend Revision Strategy

> **DO**
>
> *Jot and Blend an average of two words or phrases in your first draft.*

Teacher: We saw how easy it was for Mackenzie and Ishmael to add red words to their first drafts. They didn't add difficult words; they added words we all knew, and you all agreed that the red words made you see a better picture of their ideas. So let's get busy. I'm excited to get my red pen writing, and I'm eager to see what comes out of your red pens. We'll follow the steps that Mackenzie and Ishmael followed. (For a complete description, see *A Writing Cycle for Writer's Workshop*, p. R-15.)

- Read through your first draft, placing a slash at the end of each sentence, even if you left out the end mark.
- Count the number of sentences and place the total at the top of the draft.
- Read through your first draft a second time. Focus on the pictures that were in your mind when you wrote your first draft. Watch for the extra words and phrases that pop into your mind.
- Place a caret beneath the place in each sentence that the word or phrase fits.
- Add all of the words that come to mind, writing them in between the lines of your draft. Consult
  - The chart of Picture Killers and insert a synonym for any of these words that appear in your first draft
  - The chart of Picture Makers for words that help you add details in each of your sentences
- Add more than the expected number of words to the first sentence. This makes sure you are on track to exceed your teacher's expectation.

Setting concrete expectations for Jot and Blend: Quantify expectations for students using the Jot and Blend strategy; start with an average of two to three words per sentence. When students exceed the expectation, they shift into the world of authentic revision. Adding two or three words per sentences sounds like a reachable goal. Yet when they meet the expectation, they have added a considerable number of details (a twenty-sentence draft yields forty to sixty added words) and earns them a target ◎ (85 points). Significant revisions beyond these expectations earn students the + (100 points).

Jot and Blend may be the simplest revision strategy in the Writing Cycle framework, but that does not mean it is only for beginning writers. Check out the writing of a gifted middle school writer. Garret is making a plea to his principal for a new course in the school curriculum.

Crunch, Crunch, Munch, Munch . / That is all you hear during (some of) the class periods in a long school day. / People masticate food during class and everyone (around) that person hears it and abhors it. / Most Teachers may not take notice of the disruption, but the students usually do. / There needs to be a cooking connection class (for) this very reason. / The class will not only provide a solution to that on-going nerve-racking problem, but it will also teach the students the responsibility they need for when they are living by themselves (out) in the real world. Without it students will be as lost as a polar bear in Hawaii. /

Garret jotted down twenty-four words in his first paragraph of six sentences—four words per sentence. He continued this pace and claimed a target (85 points out of 100) for his efforts. No doubt, Garret's first draft is strong without the blended details, but it is even stronger with them. I have yet to see a first draft that did not benefit from the Jot and Blend revision strategy.

The first time your students jot and blend, invite two or three PALs to volunteer a PAL's revision that the whole class needs to hear. As a check, circulate around the room as the students revise to confirm that the PALs who have been volunteered have exemplary revisions.

> **LOOK**
>
> *Peer-assess the fit and completedness of Jot and Blend strategy used by a PAL.*

Teacher: Listen well to what Kim Cho reads so you can tell her if

- Her additions fit her first draft
- She needs to write more, write less or leave the additions as they are (see the Goldilocks rubric on page 19 of a Working Portfolio at writingtowin.com.)

Even if the class can see Kim Cho's first draft with the red revisions with a document camera, partner with her: she reads her first draft aloud, stopping at each addition, and you read the red words. When you have read through about a page of revisions, ask the class to complete these tasks:

- Raise your hand if you think the red words that I read in Kim Cho's draft fit her draft. [Tally the raised hands.]
- Raise your hand if you think that Kim Cho needs to add even more red words to her first draft. [Tally the raised hands.]
- How many say that she has written too much already? [Tally the raised hands.]
- How many say that her additions were just about right? [Tally the raised hands.]

It is important to poll the class with these points in this order. It is equally important to tally the response on the board for all to see. Figure 9.8 on page 91 shows a sample tally.

Antoine has the most additional revising to do, but he just needs to add more of what he was prompted to do in the first place. Most first-time revisers resemble Antoine; they add a little to see if it gets them by. Cortney has the biggest task. Fortunately, she has the most revision already invested in her first draft and can return to assess each addition.

On subsequent uses of Jot and Blend, students share their additions aloud in PALs of three. One PAL reads aloud the first three paragraphs of a first draft of another; a second PAL reads the red words. The writer looks on, assisting with any needed clarification. The two PALs then score their PAL's revisions with the peer revision (Goldilocks) rubric for paragraphs #1, #2 and #3. The rubric works like a charm with students and gets everyone smiling—especially you. The peer-revision rubric keeps us teachers from prompting more than three revision strategies at a time, and it gives both writer and peer reviser a sense of accomplishment.

Teacher: Conference with a revision partner to explain each of the revisions you have completed on your draft. Your partner will identify each revision in column 1 and circle his or her response to each in columns 2 and 3.

Figure 9.7 Identifying Revisions

Identify Revision	Fits the Draft?		Amount		
1. paragraph #1	(Yes)	No	Too much	About right	(Add more)
2. paragraph #2	(Yes)	No	Too much	About right	(Add more)
3. paragraph #3	(Yes)	No	Too much	(About right)	Add more

Student self-assessment for Jot and Blend: Students complete their peer assessment of the Jot and Blend strategy by judging the degree to which the writers met your stated expectation for their revision. For an expectation of two or three added words per sentence, students count the number of their sentences and multiply by two or by three to determine the target expectation for their specific first drafts. In a twenty-sentence first draft, the expectation is to blend forty to sixty words into their draft. If they have added words within that range, they assess themselves a target ◉ (85 points). If they added fewer words, they self-assess a bar ▭ (70 points). More words permit them to self-assess a plus + (100 points).

> **LEARN**
>
> *Record the elements and benefits that your class creates of strong use of the Jot and Blend revision strategy.*

Figure 9.8 Class Response

Name	Add More	Too Much	About Right	Teacher's Summary of the Response of the Class
Kim Cho	4	0	19	The class likes what you've added, but they need more of your good, vivid details. Let's see you circle places where pictures can appear.
Antoine	17	0	8	The class likes your revision the way it is, but you need to add a few more vivid details. Let's see you mark two places to add descriptive details.
Cortney	4	4	17	Some classmates think you added too much, some too little. Let's see you place two A's by sentences you can add more to. Then add two T's by sentences you can trim down.
Total	25	4	44	

The chart of student responses helps students draw conclusions about the Jot and Blend strategy. Some students whom I've met concluded that

"It was tough to add words at first."
"Then it got easier and easier."
"Every draft worth writing is worth revising [an echo of their teacher]."
"The word charts really help."
"Some red words aren't any help."
"PALs help you pick the best red words to blend."

Conclusion: Wrap up the session with a statement that everyone accepts. All first drafts can benefit from revision. The easiest revision to use is adding details. Jot down all the details that come to your mind, then decide which to keep and blend those into your final draft.

Some Thoughts about Revising First Drafts

Throughout my career, teachers have said that revision has been the hardest step of the writing process for them and their students alike. That has never been the case with the surefire revision strategies in chapters 9 through 11.

- Revision includes changing the content of first drafts, not final drafts. Revising a final draft requires rewriting that spawns new errors of usage and mechanics.

- Students select one of several first drafts to revise. If students have only two first drafts, they still have a choice.
- For a research paper, help students link 1st Draft #1, #2 and #3 together.
- After students have completed a specific revision strategy, they assess the performance of a peer using the same revision strategy.
- Students have finished revision only when they incorporate the assigned revisions (and others) into their final draft.
- Teachers use an instructional tool like a First Draft Response Form to establish the need for revision.
- Expectations for revision are always quantified to guide students through peer and self-assessment.
- Students receive full credit (in students' minds, 100 points) for revision as a task separate from other tasks in the writing process.

Looking Back

In your response journal, describe two ideas about the Jot and Blend revision strategy valuable for you as a teacher in courses that you presently teach.

Looking Ahead

Describe two places that you can use Jot and Blend or a variation of it in your coming curriculum.

Chapter 10

Fine-Tune Leads and Closes with Me

Common Core State Standards for Writing

Production and Distribution of Writing—4. Develop and strengthen writing as needed by planning, revising, editing, rewriting or trying a new approach.

"Great is the art of beginning, but greater is the art of ending."

—Henry Wadsworth Longfellow

This second revision strategy focuses on writing leads and writing closes. The Longfellow quote may mean closes are more important than leads or that they are harder to write, or both, but it is a moot point for beginning writers. Both leads and closes appear in cursory form or are nonexistent, as in Joseph's plea for a cell phone in chapter 5. Writing leads and writing closes are a pair that work together to initiate the voice, pictures and flow of students' drafts and bring them to completion. Writing leads meets the challenge of engaging readers from the beginning of a draft. Writing closes leaves readers with good memories of a draft. Writing leads answers the question, "What choices do I have to catch readers' attention and make them want to read on?" Writing closes answers the question, "What can I do to make sure that readers think and speak well of my writing once they have finished reading it?" Let's begin with the setup for teacher expectations and the student self-assessment on the next page.

Lesson with Scripting for Writing Leads

<table>
<tr>
<td valign="top">

INVITE

Select a first draft to revise.

</td>
<td valign="top">

Teacher: **Fine-tune the beginning with me.** I have a first draft here that I like a lot. In fact, I am sure that the body of my draft makes the pictures in my mind show up clearly on the page. The beginning makes me wonder,

</td>
</tr>
</table>

Figure 10.1 The Setup For Teacher Expectations

Step	Mode	Teacher Expects	Description of Topic	Points
*1st Draft #1	C	3 ¶'s	A curious animal that I discovered	85
			(Half of the points are from your prewriting and half are from your first draft.)	
*1st Draft #2	H	3 ¶'s	How to make . . .	85
*1st Draft #3	H	3 ¶'s	I'm old enough to know how to . . .	85
Revision	C	2 leads	Write leads 2 and 3 (four to six sentences) on the revision page (page 18); use the best of the three. Share with your PALs group of four.	85
			(A description of how you used this revision strategy in your first draft.)	

Figure 10.2 The Student Self-Assessment

Step	Mode	Self-Check	Description of Topic	Points
*1st Draft #1	C	◎	Amazing ducks!	92
			(Half of the points are from your prewriting and half are from your first draft.)	
*1st Draft #2	H	+	Making a scarecrow.	90
*1st Draft #3	H	+	How to ride a bike to town.	95
Revision	C	◎	I wrote leads 2 and 3. My PALs piced 3. I agree.	85
			(A description of how you used this revision strategy in your first draft.)	

though. Will my first words catch my readers' interest right away? Will my introduction keep them reading? Will they ever get to the word pictures in the second and third paragraphs that I have worked hard to create? I invite you to work on beginnings with me. I know I could use your help in responding to my draft, and I'm happy to help you, too.

<table>
<tr>
<td>

MODEL

Review a revised first draft on a previous topic that used Writing Leads.

</td>
<td>

As in earlier lessons, a simple invitation for your students to write with you suffices. Since students have written drafts on several topics before you invite them to revise, they may choose a draft that they like the best. Choosing the best draft reengages their minds squarely in their written thoughts, and they are ready to follow your invitation to fine-tune the beginning of their drafts.

</td>
</tr>
</table>

Follow your invitation to write leads with a model of three leads that you wrote. I do. Check out this character sketch of a three-toed sloth. I read each lead aloud and asked students to vote for the lead that I should use.

<table>
<tr>
<td>

Model Lead #1 (from the first draft)

</td>
<td>

The animals that I researched were called three-toed sloths. I didn't know much about them before this project. I couldn't stop reading screen after screen on the Discovery Channel Web site on the Internet. This was the most bizarre animal I had ever read about.

</td>
</tr>
<tr>
<td>

Model Lead #2 (startling facts)

</td>
<td>

My animal has three toes, but can barely use them to walk. In fact, on the ground, it takes about an hour to walk one city block. So instead of walking on the ground, it hangs in a tree all day and all night. And you think it's hard to hang from three toes all day? The female does it with all its newborn young hanging from its underbelly for about nine months.

</td>
</tr>
<tr>
<td>

Model Lead #3 (imagined wise saying)

</td>
<td>

"If you can't walk on your four feet, hang from trees. If your kids can't hang from a tree, let them hang off their mom." That's the wise advice that the animals I studied follow. Can you imagine hanging from trees day and night, never to set foot on the ground because you fear for your life? That's my animal.

</td>
</tr>
</table>

When I ask students which of my three leads catches their attention and makes them want to read the character sketch that follows, no one votes for lead #1. A lopsided majority usually selects lead #3. They explain that the first lead is plain, the second is a clear picture, but the third makes them wonder what is coming next.

My model gives you an idea for creating your own. My model may not fit your school curriculum, so your model will work best. Seven steps help your students follow your model productively. Show students each of the steps in your own writing as you ask them to follow your lead. As they write with you, the revision of their leads emerges naturally.

Steps for Revising a Lead

DO

Write two leads to your first draft using different techniques.

1. Read through a selected draft carefully from the beginning. Focus on the picture in your mind as you read your first sentence. Read on until you see the picture in your mind change; mark that spot with a slash of red ink. Remember you are marking off the first picture, not the first sentence as you did in Jot and Blend (chapter 9).

2. Draw a line from the top of the slash to the right margin and from the bottom of the slash to the left margin. The words and sentences above the line are the first picture frame in your first draft.

3. Place a large *#1* by this frame. It is lead #1.

   Note: At step 3, give students two minutes to confer with a PAL to choose lead #1. The PALs may determine that the first picture is not actually an introduction to the draft—that the draft lacks a lead. If so, a student's lead #1 is null, and they move on to writing lead #2. The partners may also discover that the lead contains several mental pictures. It may include one or more paragraphs. Most often, lead #1 is part or all of a first paragraph.

4. Brainstorm with me techniques for writing an effective lead. Start with an obvious question: "Is it possible to start your first draft a different way?" With the answer yes, the writing leads strategy has launched. Admit that there are literally dozens of ways to start a draft. "Tell me some you know. As I list them on the board, write your version of the list on your paper (the top of pages 18–19 of the Working Portfolio, www.writingtowin.com)." One group of students brainstormed these techniques for writing leads:

   - Some questions
   - A quotation (like, "Life is like a box of chocolates")
   - Dialogue
   - A little story (anecdote)
   - A joke (clearly related to the main idea)
   - Surprising facts
   - A setting for the first draft (vignette)

   Make sure that the list comes exclusively from students.

5. Students may choose any of the lead techniques from the list or ones not even on the list.
6. Just beneath the list of techniques for writing leads, place a *2*, then write the beginning of your first draft an entirely different way—any way that is different from lead #1. You have four minutes to write four or five sentences in a paragraph. Get your pencils moving.

   Note: Help reluctant students circle a technique from the list and remind them to "get your pencils moving; the best way to think is to move your pencil and leave words on the page."

7. When time is up, say, "Finish the sentence you are writing, then move your pens and pencils down the page a few lines below lead #2 and write the words *lead #3*. Now begin writing the introduction to your draft again, in any way different from the first two leads. Go back to our class list and circle an unused technique, or come up with one on your own. Just begin your draft an entirely different way. You have four minutes. You may begin."

Setting concrete expectations for writing leads: Specify expectations for writing two additional leads: both leads #2 and #3 must be a clear example of one of the techniques we have brainstormed and contain a minimum of five sentences. When students reach these expectations, they assess themselves a target ◎ (85 points). When they write fuller examples of leads #2 and #3, they assess themselves a plus + (100 points). Students may also self-assess an "exceed" (+) when they use an additional revision strategy such as Jot and Blend on their own. When students fail to write two full leads, they assess themselves a bar ⌷ (70 points).

LOOK
Help each PAL in your group of four PALs select the best of three leads.

The first time that you use the Writing Leads strategy, ask three or four students who have written two full leads to read their three leads aloud to the class for its response.

- Mention the topic of your draft in a single sentence.
- Say, "lead #1" and read it exactly as written.
- Pause a moment. Say, "lead #2" and read it exactly as written.
- Pause a moment. Say, "lead #3" and read it exactly as written.
- Got it? No comments about your leads, just read them. Ready?

On the board, tally the votes of the whole class as you ask, "How many of you think Alexis should use lead #1? lead #2? lead #3?" Make certain all students participate and vote only once.

Third-grader Chloe of Ringgold Elementary School wrote two additional full leads to introduce her research on ducks.

Ducks are so amazing! Do you want to know more about them? Femal ducks lay about 15 eggs in spring. Duck eggs are about the same size as a chicken egg. Wow! It takes 24 days until the duck hatches. It takes 48 hours until ducklings are fully hatched. For a few days the yolk is food. If the duckling cold or wet it could die. It takes four days until the legs are fully strong. They flap ther wings to mak them stronger.

Did you know ducks eyes are protected by a thin layer of skin. That's really cool! If it eats something inedible it spits it out. Ducks have soft teeth to help them chew. Ducks are more safe in water than land. When they get older the grow white fethers. The white fethers are made up of karatin.

A femal makes her nest out of dried grass, leaves, and fluffy down. Down is what ducks have when there a duck ling. Opos I forgot to tell you what they eat. Well they eat water, weeds and outher plants. Ducks are spectaculler!

Chloe continued by reading her three leads.

Lead #1 (from first draft: direct statement)	Ducks are so amazing! Do you want to know more about them?
Lead #2 (series of questions)	Have you ever met a animal that has small dull teeth? Have you ever saw a animal that flys and swims? Have you ever heard about a animal that watches her kids until there gron ups.
Lead #3 (startling facts)	My animal has a pice of skin on it's eyes. My animal is safer in water than land. If my animal eats something inedible it spits it out.

Chloe's classmates voted 0–22–5 for leads #1, #2 and #3, respectively; they were decisive, and they knew why. One classmate explained, "Lead #2 was full of suspense." Another said, "Lead #2 sounds like the best story." A third student offered, "Lead #3 sounded like other animals in the water."

After three classmates presented their three leads for whole class response, they moved into their cooperative PALS of four students. Ryan caught onto the expectations right away. After reading his first draft aloud to his small group, he read his three leads.

Lead #1 (one question and a direct statement)	Have you ever seen a jellyfish? You can see them in every ocean in the world!
Lead #2 (startling facts)	You can see right through this animal. This animal has two eyes you can't see. This animal is squishy and has no bones.
Lead #3 (series of questions)	Have you ever run from an animal in the water? Have you ever been scared by an animal that looks like a bubble? Have you ever been stung by such a strange animal?

His small group was evenly divided between lead #2 and lead #3. One student said, "Leads #2 and #3 made me wonder what the animal was." The group agreed: "Lead #1 was a good try but kind of boring." One student said, "Lead #1 didn't make me want to read anymore about jellyfish. I thought I knew about them, but I didn't."

Figure 10.3 Class Response

Student's Name	Lead #1	Lead #2	Lead #3
Chloe	0	22	5
Ryan	1	14	12
Ms. Beasley	1	13	13
Totals	2	34	55

That's third grade. All of the students chose one of two strategies that Ms. Beasley helped them brainstorm: 1) a series of questions and 2) startling facts. When students refine two strategies for writing leads, their next year's teachers will have a strong foundation for revision on which to build.

For a final look at students writing leads, let's visit a class of sixth-graders. As you would expect, their leads are more varied in strategy and length. After requiring her students to use the Writing Leads revision strategy several times, Ms. McNierney of Swannanoa Valley Montessori School received most interesting revisions. The essays were arguments for or against the presence of technology in the lives of students. Presented here are two strong writers on opposite sides of the issue. Ellie felt her lead #1 was just fine as it was, and even identified the technique as "surprising fact or statistic." She saw no reason to take four minutes to write four or five new sentences in an opening paragraph, but knew that was the expectation for her self-assessment. She sighed and went to work on lead #2, feeling quite pleased. Then she heard that lead #3 was part of the expectation; she sighed again and raised her voice—and copped an attitude—in her writing. After she read her dramatic final sentence, the class broke into laughter and scattered applause; it seemed that technology is really necessary!

Lead #1 (from first draft: surprising fact)	Hey, PEOPLE! Without technology we would have millions of people dying every year.
Lead #2 (famous quote and series of questions)	"One small step for man, one giant leap for mankind." This quote only supports my totally awesome reasons why technology ROCKS! From the discovery of fire to the first manned space shuttle, technology has only made our lives better. How would you like to live with no running water, no heat, no microwaves, no grocery stores, no pre-packaged ground beef, no AC, no medicine, no clothing stores, no toilets! I would die!
Lead #3 (prediction or warning)	WARNING: No Technology Zone. Enter with care. Tresspassers will be eaten alive by wild animals. Thanks to tranquilizer darts and cars, this warning will never actually exist. No technology? Do you want to DIE?!?!?? Without medicine, I'm betting our class would be a lot smaller. Actually, without paper mills and bulldozers and math and geometry and building materials, we wouldn't have a SCHOOL! Without technology, everybody in this class would be mud-covered, pig-farmig illiterates who daily butcher the concept of grammar.

The class was going to support her lead #3—until Ms. Nierney's quick response. "Hmm, Ellie, the two pig farmers I know here in Asheville have master's degrees in microbiology; shall I invite them to our class for a science event?" Red-faced, Ellie quipped, "Oops, blew that one, didn't you El?" and went to work on reining in her writing voice. When Ms. McNierney polled the students, they unanimously chose lead #2. I can't think of a better way to have diffused the uncorked attitude of lead #3.

On the other hand, Rachel's two leads present a very different voice than her lead #1. Notice that she doesn't play her hand so early in the draft with them, either. After hearing leads #2 and #3, the readers weren't certain how she would answer the prompt, Technology is/is not really necessary!

Lead #1 (from first draft: direct statement)	I think technology is not nessasary. Every day most people either stare at the computer or at the TV, but they both rot your brain.
Lead #2 (startling facts)	TECHNOLOGY IS NOT THAT NESASARY FOR KIDS. I mean there are so many kids and teenagers who just stare at the TV all day. They rot their brains. I'm not saying I don't do this either because I am a kid, too. I'm just saying it's a problem in America. In Africa kids do important work for their families. Here kids watch TV and computer screens.
Lead #3 (anecdote)	Ahhhhhhhhhhhhhh! My brain is rotting! "Why?" you ask. Well, because kids like me in America rot our brains by watching TV. What? You think I'm crazy? Well, you go right ahead a rot your brain if you like. Don't listen to me, but don't tell me I didn't warn you because I did. Ahhhhhhhhh! Mad children in America are attacking me. "Hey, just because I warned you that you might rot your brains doesn't mean you can chase me. Help! Somebody, HHHEEELLLPPP!"

The class applauded again; this time they evenly divided between voting for lead #2 and lead #3. Rachel seemed pleased that she had two strong possible leads for creating her final draft at the end of the week. She'd have a couple of nights to think about it before she had to make this decision.

LEARN

Record elements and benefits that your class creates of strong use of the Writing Leads revision strategy.

Student self-assessment: For the Writing Leads strategy, students assess the degree to which they met your stated expectation for their Writing Leads strategy. They need to complete three robust, quality leads. Each lead needs to be a clear example of a technique their class brainstormed. When each lead shows definite potential for reaching readers as an introduction to their draft, they assess themselves a target ◎ (85 points). If they revise less, they self-assess a bar ⊜ (70 points). To self-assess a plus + (100 points) for revision, students need to apply two revision strategies. Full use of the two strategies presented in *Writer's Workshop for the Common Core*—Jot and Blend (chapter 9) and Writing Leads (chapter 10)—help a student exceed your expectations.

Every group of students who uses Writing Leads with me blurt out conclusions before I ask for them. Get positioned to chart their comments about writing leads. Be sure to write precisely what you hear them say. Some students have concluded that

> "A lead has to be more than one sentence long."
> "We always liked leads #2 or #3 the best. Does everybody?"
> "Nobody chooses the first lead." This conclusion may spark the reading of a lead #1 from a student who thinks her lead #1 is her best. On rare occasions, the class agrees.
> "The more times you write the beginning, the better it gets."
> "It takes work to get readers' attention."

Conclusion: Allow students to reach their own conclusions, but wrap up the session with a consensus statement like, "All writers need to revise their leads. Sometimes they stay with lead #1 and change it a little. Most of the time, they find a better way to engage their readers by starting their draft an entirely different way." (**Note:** When a student chooses lead #1, help them agree in front of their peers that writing leads #2 and #3 was necessary to see how strong lead #1 was. It is critical to remind students that all writers revise.)

A side effect of inviting students to write leads with you is that you receive honest help in fine-tuning leads in your own writing. Most of my drafts get shared with several classes. My sketch of the three-toed sloths has met over a dozen audiences. Without hesitation, the last group of twenty-five fifth-graders registered their preference: 3–6–16. It finally dawned on me that lead #3 foreshadowed the major theme of the draft. While animals do unusual things, they absolutely do what is best for themselves; that's my kind of animal.

Combinations of Revision Strategies

Writing leads is best combined with another revision strategy to revise a complete draft. The possible combinations include the revision strategies such as those covered in *A Writing Cycle for Writer's Workshop* (pp. R-1 through R-22). The revisions here in chapters 9–11 come from that source and work well in combination.

- Writing Leads: Combining Sentences (chapter 11) for drafts that contain specific word choices but have unevenly crafted sentences.
- Writing Leads: Jot and Blend (chapter 9) in a well-organized draft that needs help in establishing a consistent voice or adding crisp details throughout.

A short conference with groups of students or a written teacher commentary (see the First Draft Response Form, chapter 9) leads students to choose effective combinations of revision strategies themselves.

Writing Closes

Once you succeed at prompting your students to write leads, you are only a step away from prompting them to write effective closes. The revision strategy Writing Closes mirrors Writing Leads. They both ask students to

- Identify key pictures in their drafts.
- Write two additional versions of part of their drafts.
- Receive immediate help from PALS in choosing their best lead or close.
- Combine their lead or close with another revision strategy to revise the draft completely.
- Write three quality leads or closes to receive full credit for revision.

The two strategies parallel each other, but the purposes for writing a lead and a close in writing a draft are quite different.

1. Leads engage readers. If students do not engage their readers, the readers never read the close.
2. When a lead does its work effectively and the body of a draft contains effective voice, pictures and flow, the close must be ready to do its job also. An effective close prompts readers to act—maybe even to tell others about the writing they just read. The following examples for writing a close are unique to writing closes.

   - **A prediction:** If you decide to swim where jellyfish live, you will see them. Count on it. When one touches you, it will sting. The more the animal gets tangled up with you, the more it will sting. You and the jellyfish will feel under attack. The safest choice is to keep your distance and enjoy the sight of this unusual creature.
   - **A warning:** When you swim where you know jellyfish live, forget about horseplay and chasing friends around. You can still have fun in the ocean on a raft or in shallow water with the tide flowing out. But do not take chances. Most encounters with jellyfish are harmless. But some are not. Be safe, not sorry.
   - **A call to action:** When you spot a jellyfish in the water, move, but move slowly. Turn sideways to the animal and move slowly away sideways. This way, you won't create a wake in the water and bring the jellyfish right along with you. Jellyfish cannot give chase.
   - **A spirited summary of the main idea or ideas:** Enjoy these unique creatures. Most important for you to know when you are surprised by one is they have no brain and cannot move on their own. There are many unusual features to admire, so stand back and see if you can find the eyes, which are nearly invisible, and an appendage that looks like a bell. Then check out some of the internal body

parts—the stomach is especially easy to see and may contain a fish that was eaten for supper.

Students soon learn that all first drafts can benefit from a quick but serious look at leads and closes, even if the lead they select was part of their first draft or a combination of two leads.

After a trip to the station of leads and closes, students approach their final drafts with confidence. Confidence as writers goes a long way toward accelerating ongoing improvements in student writing.

On the next page is an example of how a teacher used the station for Writing Leads and Closes for a real purpose in her school. She placed three opening paragraphs (leads) to a recommendation she wrote to her school's leadership team. The draft requested that grant monies be spent on setting up learning stations like hers throughout the school. In modeling authentic writing for students, it is important to go beyond writing with students on the same writing topic prompt as they write. Why not bring them into the realm of authentic school writing for an actual purpose? Which lead hooks your interest?

Which Lead Hooks Your Interest?

We teachers are often asked to recommend ways to improve teaching and learning here at Sinclair Elementary. Often that includes the need to spend funds budgeted for school improvement. I have been asked to recommend and convince the school's leadership team to purchase the tables, chairs and project display boards for a writing station like the station for Writing Leads and Closes in our classroom.

Help me out. Read through the following three leads and tell me which one you think will engage the leadership team and convince them to create writing stations in every classroom.

Lead #2

Members of the leadership team:

Charlie predicted how much money we could raise in a closing paragraph of his science project. Lakisha rewrote her opening paragraph that judges cited as the winning feature of her essay on gender-segregated classes by the Young Georgia Authors competition. Won Mo's opening sentences persuaded Ms. Smith to read and select his idea for the only field trip fifth-grade was permitted this year. All of these self-initiated revisions happened at the makeshift station for Writing Leads and Closes. Just imagine the impact if every classroom for grades 3 through 5 had one of these magical stations.

Lead #1

Members of the leadership team:

I am writing to recommend the use of $2,000 for the purchase of tables and display boards for Writing Leads and Closes stations in all classrooms, grades 2 through 5. We teachers received the recommendation from a coaches' workshop in writing that convinced us of their importance.

Lead #3

Members of the leadership team:

At faculty meetings and leadership meetings, we have heard that students should work harder at learning than their teachers do at teaching. That vision is very possible at Sinclair Elementary with very few changes. We already have desks for cooperative groups; we have in-class shelves for independent reading. The next obvious step is a simple learning station for writing called Writing Leads and Closes. Let me explain.

Vote for one and explain why.

Name	Circle one	Explain
1 _____	1 2 3	_____
2 _____	1 2 3	_____
3 _____	1 2 3	_____
4 _____	1 2 3	_____
5 _____	1 2 3	_____
6 _____	1 2 3	_____
7 _____	1 2 3	_____
8 _____	1 2 3	_____
9 _____	1 2 3	_____
10 _____	1 2 3	_____

Tips for Using First Draft Response Forms

Writing teacher commentaries is often the first task in the writing process that overly busy teachers abandon. That doesn't have to be the case if you keep these tips in mind.

- Complete a First Draft Response Form for all students at the same time. Stringing the commentaries out over several days leads to changing the first commentaries after you reach the last ones.
- Quick-read a draft.
- Circle a number from 1 to 4 on the primary trait rubric so that the students receive this clear message: if I don't revise this first draft seriously, I won't be taking the grade home that I need.
- Time yourself. Take 15 minutes to group the writing by similar needs in revision.
- Place them according to the following revision codes that describe students' most urgent needs. Place students in no more than two codes.

  - Code A (Add details throughout)   Jot and Blend
  - Code B (Improve the beginning)   Writing Leads
  - Code C (Improve the closing)   Writing Closes
  - Code D (Diversity in words and sentences) Combining Sentences

- Time yourself again. Pick up the Code A stack. Take 60 seconds per student and write a one- to two-sentence commentary for each student in the group. Repeat the process with students in Codes B, C and D.

Some of your students' writing fits in all four codes. In this case, choose one code as the priority for this revision task. It is better if students complete one revision code well instead of four haphazardly. Set a timer if you must. Don't mull over each draft; it will wear you out before you are even halfway through skim-reading the drafts. Just make certain that when students follow the prompt in your commentary that their writing exceeds the standard of the current writing task.

Looking Back

In your response journal, describe two ideas about Writing Leads and Writing Closes that were valuable for you in a course that you teach.

Looking Ahead

In what aspects of your future curriculum will Writing Leads or Writing Closes increase effective student learning?

Chapter 11

Combine Sentences with Me

> ### Common Core State Standards for Writing
>
> Production and Distribution of Writing—5. Develop and strengthen writing as needed by ... revising, editing, rewriting ...
>
> ### Common Core State Standards for Language
>
> Conventions of Standard English—1. Demonstrate command of the conventions of standard English grammar and usage when writing or speaking.
>
> Conventions of Standard English—2. Demonstrate command of the conventions of standard English capitalization, punctuation and spelling when speaking and writing.
>
> Vocabulary Acquisition and Use—6. Acquire and use accurately grade-appropriate general academic and domain-specific words and phrases, including those that signal contrast, addition and other logical relationships (e.g., however, although, nevertheless, similarly, moreover, in addition).

"Civilization's greatest single invention is the sentence. In it, we can say anything."

—John Banville

"A perfectly healthy sentence . . . is extremely rare."

—Benjamin Franklin

The third look at revision may be the most important. It focuses on sentences, and it offers the revision strategy that replaces most of the class time devoted to teaching language skills in isolation. Most people don't think as highly of the sentence as contemporary British novelist John Banville. Nor do they think of healthy sentences as unattainable as Ben Franklin. Yet classroom practices lead us to think so; in U.S. public and private schools, the sentence (and especially its conventions) receives more class time than any other piece of the language arts curriculum. The result? Up until now, scores of writing style (sentence variety and word choice) have not moved upward in three decades of testing written expression. Steve Graham of Vanderbilt University says that it is the way we ask students to study, experience and use them in language studies and writing. In *Writing Next*, his staff recognized sentence-combining practice as the language skill that impacts scores of written expression most significantly. In the five rigorous classroom studies his team reviewed, the positive statistical impact was well above the level of significance. In the eighteen qualified studies of direct instruction in language, only three posted a significant positive effect; five showed no effect, and ten showed a significantly negative effect. So here's the quick-and-easy contrast between sentence-combining practice and direct instruction in language skills.

- Sentence-combining teaches grammatical patterns by conditioning students to combine simple sentences into more mature Standard Written English sentence patterns.
- Direct instruction in grammatical patterns requires students to analyze and take sentences apart.
- Teaching grammar terms after students have acquired the grammatical pattern in sentence-combining practice allows students to learn the language of grammar more deeply than direct instruction.
- Direct instruction often presents sentences filled with errors for students to correct that follow patterns they have heard and used since birth.
- Sentence-combining puzzles include sentences with no errors. They include only patterns of Standard Written English.

In addition, combining sentences parallels what happens in the human brain when we write. It is no surprise that sentence-combining practice is the most effective strategy of language study. Research data since 1968 reports this fact in action research studies with students from first grade to graduate school and from students with special needs to gifted students.

This instructional strategy for boosting scores of writing style has been around since 1965. Psycholinguist John Mellon of Harvard University taught students to combine sentences and name the combinations they created based on Noam Chomsky's transformational-generative grammar. Mellon found that with sentence-combining practice, students' writing grew significantly in syntactic maturity, showing two years growth in a single year. From the sentence-combining research of the next ten years, we learned that, indeed, sentence-combining practice transferred mature sentence patterns immediately to student writing. And the presence of sentence-combining practice rings positive for twenty-first-century student writers, as indicated in the research of Graham, Saddler, et al. (2005, 2007, 2009).

One sentence-combining technique that applies directly to the revision of a first draft includes signals placed in parentheses at the end of the signal sentence they affect. There are fewer than ten rules for signals, and they have no exceptions. Keeping exception to rules to a minimum in the study of language is a real plus. The following rule results in the creation of both complex and compound sentences (*Sentence Building*, level v, pp. 12–14).

Move signal words in parentheses to the front of the sentences that they follow. Then add the signal sentence to the base sentence.

Base sentence	**Jessie flopped back into bed.**
Signal sentence	The announcer predicted rain all day. (after)
Combined sentence	Jessie flopped back into bed **after** the announcer predicted rain all day.

Base sentence	**The girls went to lunch early.**
Signal sentence	The boys waited until almost 1:00 PM to eat. (, and)
Combined sentence	The girls went to lunch early, **and** the boys waited until almost 1:00 P.M. to eat.

After a lesson of eight to twelve of these puzzles like those in the first example, teachers present the *know-about knowledge* of the grammatical pattern. That's it.

- Practice the grammatical pattern until students create them automatically.
- Present the names for the pattern and its parts when students have a specific mental construct in their heads that need a name.

In order for the grammatical pattern to transfer to students' independent writing, they need to write and speak the combinations of eight or more puzzles in a lesson that repeat the pattern with different ideas using

Oral practice:	Students speak the combined sentence in a group so teachers can see that all have acquired the pattern.
Kinesthetic practice:	With a hand or body movement, students signal each change required in combining the sentences orally.
Written practice:	Students write the combined sentences independently.

Another rule covers the fate of repeated words in signal sentences. Students may leave the second occurrence of the repeated word out, as with "the rabbits" in the first puzzle below. If deleting the repeated word doesn't make sense, students replace the repeated word with a pronoun. It is remarkable to see students who meet sentence-combining practice for the first time delete and replace repeated words accurately from the get-go.

If there are repeated words in the signal sentence, leave them out of the combined sentence.

Base sentence	**The hawk swooped down on the rabbits**
Signal sentence	The rabbits scrambled for cover. (that)
Combined sentence	The hawk swooped down on the rabbits that scrambled for cover.

Base sentence	**Aaron tried on the shirt.**
Signal sentence	Aaron made the shirt in Family Studies II. (that)
Combined sentence	Aaron tried on the shirt that he made in Family Studies II.

Although describing different sentence-combining strategies requires serious effort, performing the combinations for students does not. Once they understand how a signal works, they combine with alertness and speed. They see each new exercise as a puzzle and fall prey to its allure. Here are the first four puzzles of a lesson with signals.

Sentence Building
(Oral, then Written Practice)

1. **The immigrants had no money to their names. (Although)**
   The immigrants were soon self-supporting. (,)
   Although the immigrants had no money to their names, they were soon self-supporting.

2. **Leroy was visiting a dozen college campuses. (While)**
   Le Won received three scholarships in the mail. (,)
   While Leroy was visiting a dozen college campuses, Le Won received three scholarships in the mail.

3. **Our teacher takes a go-cart from the parking lot.**
   Our teacher could use the exercise. (**even though**)
   Our teacher takes a go-cart from the parking lot even though he/she could use the exercise.

4. **The lake is stocked with fish. (Since)**
   The lake is behind the school.
   Trolling and bobbing for fish is a PE elective. (,)
   Since the lake behind the school is stocked with fish, trolling and bobbing for fish is a PE elective.

The complete lesson is viewable at www.writingtowin.com.

> **Grammatical pattern practiced:** The puzzles present adverb clauses. The signal sentence joins a previous sentence with a subordinate conjunction (such as *because, if, even though* or *although*), making it a dependent clause (unable to stand alone). Since the clause modifies (describes) the verb in the base sentence, it is an adverbial clause.

Lesson with Scripting for Combining Sentences

INVITE
Select a first draft to revise.

Teacher: **Work on our styles of writing with me.** I see from reviewing your first drafts that parts of your writing resemble parts of mine. Like me, you write short, simple sentences so your pencil can keep up with your mind. When we draft our thoughts the first time, we are writing for ourselves. When we reread our first drafts, we see the pictures in our minds again, but few others will. So we need to work on making our mental pictures clearer for our readers. Work with me on combining some of the sentences so that the pictures sharpen for our readers.

MODEL
Review a revised first draft using Combining Sentences on a previous topic.

Look at the writing of sixth-grader Lucy from Monticello, Georgia as she summarizes an article for her science class on the prospects of robots in the lives of Americans in the future. Her first draft is nearly devoid of her personal style and the energy of an exciting breakthrough—robots in our houses! Notice what a difference combining sentences makes. Lucy combined the sentences that she marked for that purpose.

Setting Concrete Expectations for Combining Sentences in a Draft

Circle five or six pairs of sentences that would be better off combined. Then combine four of them into more mature and informative sentences. It's fine to insert additional words and phrases that help paint a

First Draft	Revision
Soon Robots Will Be at Your Service	**Soon Robots Will Be at Your Service**
These days robots are not very strong. They can't do very much for us. In the future we want them to be able to do more things. It would be nice if they got our breakfast for us. How about cleaning the car? Doing the dishes would be nice. I hope that they will do a lot for us but not so much that it makes us lazy. We could get real clumsy.	These days robots are not very strong. They can't do very much for us. In the future we want them to be able to do more things. It would be nice if they got our breakfast for us, <u>cleaned the family car and even washed the dishes.</u> I hope that they will do a lot for us but not so much that it makes us lazy. We could get real clumsy.
Joseph Bosworth is president of Robot Sciences of Golden, Colorado. He thinks that robots can change our lives. It will take fifteen to twenty years. He is sure it will come. Research in medicine will play a big part. So will the technology in Disney World called animatronics. Robots will have artificial limbs, too. They are made for people now. They will be on the robots of the future. I think movie producers might be able to make a show of just robots. Only some of this is for sure.	Joseph Bosworth <u>is president of Robot Sciences of Golden, Colorado and</u> thinks that robots can change our lives <u>in</u> fifteen to twenty years for sure. Research in medicine <u>and</u> the technology in Disney World called animatronics will play a big part. Robots will have artificial limbs <u>like the ones</u> made for people now. I think movie producers might be able to make a show of just robots.

combine (first paragraph)

combine *combine* *combine* (second paragraph)

<table>
<tr><th>DO</th><td rowspan="1">more vivid picture of your thoughts. When you reach either of these expectations, you assess yourself a target ⊙ (85 points). For exceeding the expectations, you self-assess a plus + (100 points); for missing expectations, a bar ▭ (70 points).</td></tr>
</table>

DO

Combine 3–4 pairs of sentences that you circled in your first draft.

more vivid picture of your thoughts. When you reach either of these expectations, you assess yourself a target ⊙ (85 points). For exceeding the expectations, you self-assess a plus + (100 points); for missing expectations, a bar ▭ (70 points).

A Younger Writer

From Jeffersonville Elementary, third-grader Jeffrey crafted, without assistance from anyone, an engaging, imaginative story about a pet monkey that met an untimely death. From his first draft, you can feel the energy of his narrative, but the immature sentence patterns show that he is quite young. His teacher prompted him to revise by combining sentences. The difference that sentence study made for Jeffrey when he followed the prompt of this concrete revision strategy is obvious. He went beyond his teacher's expectations.

First Draft	Revision
An Explorer Monkey	An Explorer Mondey
Once upon a time there lived a monkey. He was black and brown. They called him Mike Monkey. He just died five months ago. He died because I let him eat poison ivy. Mike Monkey was a lively little fellow. He like to eat. He like to play and sleep, too. The thing he liked most was to explore. Mike liked to play tag through the trees with other monkeys. He even liked to race humans. He like to eat chicken. He likes to eat bananas, paper and tangarines. He sleeps a lot.	Once upon a time there lived a monkey that was black and brown. They called him Mike Monkey. He just died five months ago because I let him eat poison ivy. Mike Monkey was a lively little fellow. He liked to eat, play and sleep, but the thing he liked most was to explore. Mike liked to play tag through the trees with other monkeys. He even liked to race humans. He likes to eat chicken, bananas, paper and tangarines and he sleeps a lot.
He explored the Great Wall of China. He explored the Taj Mahal. He explored the Washington Memorial and the Ifle Tower in Paris. Mike wears a beige hat. He wears his hair in a very, very long tail. So I have been looking for him ever since. You will notice him. He can talk. He's talking to animals right now. I hear him. I found him. I see him.	He explored the Great Wall of China, the Taj Mahal, the Washington Memorial and the Ifle Tower in Paris. Mike wears a beige hat and his hair is in a very, very long tail. So I have been looking for him ever since. You will notice him because he can talk. He's talking to animals right now. I hear him and I found him. Can you see him?
"Come here, Mike. I've got some bananas for you. Come down Mike." "Okay I'm coming," Mike said.	"Come here, Mike. I've got some bananas for you. Come down Mike." "Okay I'm coming," Mike said.
He kept eating his banana. I grabbed him and went home. When we got home we played tag. We raced, too. When we were racing he jumped off course. He landed on a tree. That's when he ate a poisonous fruit. He died. Now I have a new pet. His name is Donny Dog.	While he kept eating his banana, I grabbed him and went home. When we got home we played and raced. When we were racing he jumped off course and landed on a tree. That's when he ate a poisonous fruit and died. Now I have a new pet. His name is Donny Dog.

combine {
combine {
combine {
combine {
combine {
combine {
combine {
combine {

Although there is more than combining sentences that could have been revised in his first draft, Jeffrey does a solid job of combining the sentences that he circled in his first draft. After he shared his revised draft aloud with the class, I asked him to talk about the combining sentences strategy he use. "I like using the *while* and *because* signals the best." His revision illustrates the point that know-how knowledge precedes know-about knowledge (chapter 4). Even though his teacher had used the label "adverb clause" for the signals he likes, *adverb clause* was not active in his know-about vocabulary just yet. For sure, a number of the combined sentences include *and*, but the draft reads more smoothly. There are other days and other drafts on which to practice and refine this and other revision strategies.

> **LOOK**
>
> *Peer-assess the fit and completedness of inserting words/phrases used by your PAL.*

When the students have finished the prompted revision task for combining sentences #1, say this to them:

Teacher: Take turns reading your first drafts aloud with your PAL, showing how you inserted descriptive terms before and after the circled nouns. For each noun that you have modified, complete the following table:

Figure 11.1 PAL Responses

Ask your PAL:	Write your PAL's response in the margin.		
Does the combination fit?	It fits.		Does not fit.
Do the combinations improve the draft?	No.	Almost.	Indeed it does.

> **LOOK**
>
> *Peer-assess the fit and completedness of Combining Sentences by your PAL.*

When the students have finished the prompted revision task for combining sentences, say this:

Teacher: Show the combined sentences to your PAL for a response. Write what your PAL says in the margin by each combination.

"Combined sentences improve the pictures."
"Need to combine this one another way."
"Add more to this combination."

Student self-assessment: Students assess the degree to which they met your expectations for combining sentences.

Figure 11.2 Student Self-Assessment

Expectation #2	Self-Assessment
Combined four or more groups of sentences together successfully.	+ (100 points)
Combined two or three groups of sentences together successfully.	◎ (85 points)
Combined sentences together unsuccessfully.	⊜ (70 points)

> **LEARN**
>
> *Record the elements and benefits that your class creates of strong use of the Combining Sentences revision strategy.*

Students in a third-grade classroom observed the following about combining sentences as a revision strategy:

"Some of my sentences looked like a puzzle in the green book (*Sentence Building*)."

"Writing needs lots of details."

"Longer sentences are better." [For third-graders, this is mostly true.]

"Combining sentences makes a better story."

"Big sentences are made of little sentences."

"Signal words let you combine sentences." [I see why they think so.]

Conclusion: Ask students to respond to the statement, "Longer sentences are not always better sentences." Lead them in discussing the difference between combining sentences with *and* and function words like *of, after, because, if, when, with, to* and *that.* You needn't talk about these latter words as prepositions or conjunctions before you can expect your students to use them successfully.

A Parting Strategy for Revision

Most of your writers need to add words and phrases in revision. At the same time, they need to consider deleting words that are used too often. For readers, words repeated unnecessarily jump off the page at readers and maim or kill the voice of the writing. Let's call the strategy Spotting Weasel Words. These words add little substance to drafts and sap the writing of its energy or special character. Fifth-grader Melvin wrote an expository first draft about tornadoes the day before I demonstrated the Spotting Weasel Words strategy in his class. Light-heartedly, I announced that first drafts with an extremely high number of repeated words are diagnosed as "having a case of the *woulds* or *wents*"—or whatever word appeared too often. Melvin's teacher had fun diagnosing several students' first drafts thereafter and celebrating how easy it was to fix the problem. Here's Melvin's first draft, on which he circled every appearance of the word *can*, and the "de-weaseled" version that he presented with a broad smile. He also made additional changes with a PAL before he wrote a final draft. He promised he would never use a word that much ever again. He probably won't.

First Draft	"De-weaseled" Draft

A tornadoe can mess up anything. If it is an animal or a person it will die. Tornadoes can kill up to 1,000-2,000 people a day. A tornado can get very powerful. It can suck everything in its path. A tornadoes can cause a lot of dammeg one at a time.
 	
   A tornodoe can be very hurtful. It can come out of nowhere. A torndoe is made up of strong air. Most of the time it can start from the ground. Sometimes it can start from air.
	A tornadoe <u>knows how to</u> mess up anything. If ~~it is~~ an animal or a person <u>that gets in its way</u> it will die. Tornadoes ~~can~~ kill up to 1,000-2,000 people a day. A tornado can become ~~get~~ very powerful. <u>Then it</u> ~~can~~ suck<u>s up</u> everything in its path. <u>T</u>ornadoes ~~can~~ cause a lot of dammeg one at a time.
	
	   A tornodoe ~~can~~ <u>has the power to</u> be very hurtful. It ~~can~~ comes out of nowhere. A tornadoe is made up of strong air<u>, and</u> <u>m</u>ost of the time it ~~can~~ start<u>s</u> from the ground. Sometimes it ~~can~~ start<u>s</u> from air.

I recall the way that I prompted Melvin to share his improved draft aloud with the class. PALs read their first drafts aloud to one another and responded by pointing out words that were either listed on the Picture Killers chart or used more than four or five times for the writer to circle. The PALs had 5 minutes to change the circled words to more vivid word choices with the aid of a thesaurus or other word study tool. When 5 minutes was up, I asked, "How many heard your PAL read a revised draft that was impressively different?" Melvin's PAL raised her hand, and Melvin was one of three to share. The class broke into warm applause for each. I had no trouble joining in on the celebration. A concrete, specific and easy-to-understand revision strategy had triumphed again.

Let's Have a Little Fun

Listed in Figure 11.3 are twenty-four language rules that I have heard people say are very important. Notice that every rule is written so it breaks the rule that it presents. Go ahead and laugh a little—or a lot. Then mark whether the rule is

- Very important for writers to remember
- Not important
- Important sometimes

Figure 11.3 Important Language Rules?

No.	The Rule	Always Important?	Minor?	Some-times?
1	Verbs has to agree with their subjects.	X		
2	Prepositions are not good to end sentences with.		X	
3	Avoid clichés like the plague. They are old hat.	X		
4	Also, always avoid aggravating alliteration.	X		
5	Be more or less specific.	X		
6	Parenthetical remarks (however important) are (usually) unnecessary.	X		
7	And don't start a sentence with a conjunction.			X
8	Also too, never, ever repeat unnecessarily.	X		
9	No sentence fragments. Ever.			X
10	Contractions aren't necessary and shouldn't be used.		X	
11	Foreign words and phrases are never *apropos*.		X	
12	Don't use no double negatives.	X		
13	Shun ampersands & abbreviations, etc.	X		
14	One-word sentences? Eliminate.			X
15	The passive voice is to be ignored.	X		
16	Eliminate commas, that are, not necessary.	X		
17	Never use a big word when a miniature one suffices.	X		
18	Kill all exclamation points!!!	X		
19	Use words correctly, irregardless of how others use them.	X		
20	Understatement is probably somewhat better than exaggeration.	X		
21	Use the apostrophe in it's proper place and omit it when its not needed.	X		
22	If you've heard it once, you've heard it a thousand times: resist hyperbole; not one writer in a million uses it correctly.	X		
23	Puns are for children, not groan readers.	X		
24	Exaggeration is a billion times worse than understatement.	X		

Looking Back

In your response journal, describe the value of combining sentences and spotting "weasel words" for you as a teacher in courses that you presently teach.

Looking Ahead

How can lessons, chapters or units coming up in your curriculum invite you to prompt your students to combine sentences and excise weasel words?

Chapter 12

Proofread a Final Draft with Me

> ### Common Core State Standards for Writing
>
> Production and Distribution of Writing—5. Develop and strengthen writing as needed by planning, revising, editing, rewriting or trying a new approach.
>
> ### Common Core State Standards for Language
>
> Conventions of Standard English—1. Demonstrate command of the conventions of standard English grammar and usage when speaking and writing.
>
> Conventions of Standard English—2. Demonstrate command of the conventions of standard English capitalization, punctuation and spelling when speaking and writing.

"I was working on the proof of one of my poems all the morning and took out a comma. In the afternoon I put it back again."

—Oscar Wilde

In chapters 6–11, you invited students to follow well-tested strategies for starting and improving the voice, pictures and flow of first drafts. They followed the strategy, your model and the responses of their peers. All students returned to the pictures they had in their minds when they wrote their first drafts. They tried their revisions out on an audience *after* they had completed a revision strategy. Based on the response of PALs or small groups of peers, they created a final draft, jotting and blending additional details to create a final draft. The focus now shifts to your students' final drafts.

It is time to help them to plumb the powers of copyediting and ensure that the final draft makes a good first and lasting impression on their readers. I don't use the word *editing* with students since it doesn't mean much to many of them. *Proofreading* conveys "slow reading"—precisely what we need students to do. The pacing for a week of proofreading follows (Figure 12.1). The week of proofreading parallels the routine of previous weeks of the Writing Cycle. Monday and Wednesday focus on students' work on a proofreading strategy like the Proofreading Triads presented here. Tuesday provides time for you to work with Proofreading Triads that need coaching while other students engage in a word study. Thursday provides time for sentence study, and Friday closes the proofreading week with small and whole-group author's chair. I chose to show you Proofreading Triads strategy since it works best for me. Other equally concrete, specific and easy-to-understand strategies appear in *A Writing Cycle for Writer's Workshop* (2011, pp. PR-10–PR-19). The most popular of these among elementary and middle school teachers is "proofreading pairs" (p. PR-11). Still, Proofreading Triads works with the greatest rigor for me.

The first time students proofread with you, start with two simple questions:

1. Are the voice and pictures in your writing clear enough to appear in your readers' minds? [After significant revision, most students feel that they are.]
2. What can keep the pictures in a final draft from moving into readers' minds?

I field responses that echo earlier emphases:

"Specific details." [We added those in revision already.]
"Not enough sentences." [We inserted those in revision, too.]
"Mistakes."
"Ah, mistakes! You mean mistakes can distract readers from seeing the pictures and hearing the voice that you intend?" There is general agreement that they can.
"Good. Now we are ready to proofread."

Here I remind students:

- They can help each other proofread even if they don't feel confident enough to do so.
- We teachers are not here to find their errors for them.
- We are here to help them become experts at finding each other's errors.

If my host teacher has previously mentioned that the students are not practiced proofreaders, I ask three questions in order for the class to reach consensus.

Tell me this about proofreading. Is it easier for you to find errors if you

- Find them yourself or let somebody else help? (Consensus on "somebody else.")

Figure 12.1 Proofreading a Writing Cycle for Writer's Workshop

Prime I (7–10 min), mini-lesson (**ML**); Prime III (15–20 min), workshop (**W**);
Prime II (7–10 min), close (**C**)

Day →		Monday	Tuesday	Wednesday	Thursday	Friday
Working Portfolio: 1st Draft # 1	**M L**	**Invite and Model** Proof-reading includes Proof-reading Triads.	**Word study:** spelling	**Invite and Model** Guide for Proofreading Triads	**Invite and Model** Model the transfer of helpful corrections to a final draft.	**Invite and Model** Weekly **Author's Chair**
	W	**Do (write)** **PALs of three proof-read** 3/4 of errors in one of their final drafts. **Teacher IDs triads** with incomplete proof-reading for small group work tomorrow.	**Do (write)** **Teacher** tutors students with incomplete proof-reading. **Word Study:** spelling within word families	**Do (write)** **PALs of three proof-read** 3/4 of errors in remaining two final drafts.	**Do (write)** **Create final draft** from first draft and revisions, making further revisions. **Sentence Study:** building noun clauses	**Look (share and respond)** Whole group **Author's Chair:** Four to five students share proof-reading changes in small groups and select one to share with the whole class and post on class display.
	C	**Look (share and reflect)** **Author's chair close** (5–7 min): students share their written task with their PALs to receive coaching with a specific response strategy.				**Learn (explain)** Whole group lists elements and benefits of Proof-reading Triads.

- Have one somebody or two somebodies help? (Consensus on "two.")
- Have somebody read your final draft silently or aloud? (Consensus on "aloud.")

So the rationale for proofreading in groups of three is set.

> **Caveat:** Listen carefully to how students answer these questions: some students will respond to a different question than the one you are asking. Some students simply do not want their final drafts read aloud. Taking the time to overcome the anxiety of having their final drafts read aloud for error identification is worth the effort.

Moving on, I present Proofreading Triads with the fervor of a salesperson.

> You're going to love proofreading in threes. Two of your peers will fix most of your errors without making a single mark on your paper, and it won't cost you a dime. Is that a good deal, or what? All corrections made on each other's final drafts must be made on a proofing strip.

At this point I lead the class in tearing a clean sheet of notebook paper in half (hot-dog style) and attaching each half to the first two pages of the final draft with a tiny piece of tape. The page and proofing strip do not overlap, permitting the students to fold the strips neatly behind each page upon completion. See Figure 12.2 for an example.

The last points I cover before I let students work in threes are foundational for proofreading. As I write them on the board, they record them in the note-taking section of their class notebooks.

> Writers proofread only final drafts, not first drafts.

Exception: You may ask student to proofread the two first drafts in a Writing Cycle that they chose not to revise for practice with language conventions. Practice in the context of their own writing trumps language worksheets of canned sentences.

> Writers proofread for writing conventions (mechanics and usage), not the voice, pictures or flow of writing. The time for addressing those traits of writing has passed.

Figure 12.2 Sample Proofing Strip

Final Draft	Proofing Strip
Writer—Warren Combs	Caller—Ho Kim Fixer—Ramone
This past April as a celebration of a wedding anniversary, I drove with my wife, Arnelle, through the Yakima valley of Washington where I spent most of the first thirteen years of my life. Mt. Adams imposed itself from the west. Arnelle's response was immediate, "Now, that's a mountain." We focused on that majestic, dormant, snow-cap volcanoe at each stop on our trip through the lower valley of fruit orchards, vineyards, hop yards and struggling farm towns. I was shocked by the size of the house at 703 S. Toppenish Ave. that I called home up through the 3rd grade. I remembered a good-size front lawn that served as a infield diamond for endless games of softball. But now the tiny patches of grass on either side of a short path from sidewalk to porch appeared too small for a lemonade stand, much less fast-paced innings of ball.	

(Tape)

Note 1: Students view the proofing strip as protection against copying the final draft over. Teachers view it as an accurate error profile for each student and a quick check of the percent of errors corrected by the triad. The strip is a win for teachers and students.

Note 2: Students receive a cooperative group grade for proofreading: a plus + (100 points), a target ◎ (85 points), a bar ⊟ (70 points) or other values you choose. Anxious proofreaders feel the support of a group on a task that isn't their forte.

Note 3: Students have only 15 minutes per draft to find and correct errors. Time limits prompt students to perform at their peak by telling their minds to get busy.

Exception: Students may choose to continue to revise during the focus on proofreading. If they do so, they understand they have to rewrite their final draft and run the risk of creating new errors.

> Proofreading is a group effort, even for professional writers. Proofreading Triads include a caller, a fixer and me, the writer.

Lesson with Scripting for Proofreading Final Drafts

INVITE

Join a group of three proofreading PALs.

Teacher: **Fix the minor goofs with me.** I have in my hand a final draft that makes me rather proud. I feel like it is ready to show, but I also know I am human. We writers make mistakes when we write—silly little goofs that distract readers from our meaning. So I need your help, and you can have mine. We writers are the last people to find our own mistakes, but any reader can spot mistakes in a flash. Our minds move much faster than our pens. We make mistakes trying to keep up with our minds. My final draft looks impressive from a distance, and your final drafts do, too. Yet there are little goofs waiting in there to distract readers if we don't fix them first.

Actually, I need to admit something to you [pulling a proofing strip out from behind my final draft to show that it is taped to the right-hand side]. Two fourth-grade buddies of mine helped me find and fix the errors in my writing. This is what they found. Ho Kim was the caller and Ramone was the fixer. Since I was the writer, I had a dictionary in my hand, and the three of us worked together. They helped me find and fix my minor goofs; Ho Kim and I helped Ramone fix his, and Ramone and I helped Ho Kim fix hers. We followed these rules for a Proofreading Triad, one of the proofreading strategies in *A Writing Cycle for Writer's Workshop* (p. PR-10). (See page 126, Figure 12.3 to see how the Triad helped me revise my essay.)

MODEL

Review the proofreading of a final draft by three PALs on a previous topic.

Proofreading Strategy #2: Proofreading Triads

1. Three students proofread each of their three final drafts in turn, sitting side by side so that all can see the draft easily. A proofing strip is attached to the right-hand side of each final draft. The writer's name is at the top of the final draft. His or her two proofreading partners' names are written at the top of the proofing strip next to their assigned role as caller or fixer.

2. One student, playing the role of **caller**, calls out each word individually, pronouncing each exactly as it is spelled or misspelled.

3. The second student, the **writer** of the draft, manages the dictionary or thesaurus for the triad, looking up words and the spelling of words the triad is unsure of.

4. The third student, the **fixer**, writes out the correction on the same line of the proofing strip on which the errors appear in the draft.

---

5. The teacher moves among the desks, coaching triads of students and helping them place a (+), (◎) or (⊜) at the top of the proofing strips according to the announced criteria. For example, a (+) means that the triad of students found almost all of the designated errors and corrected them on the proofing strip; (◎) means that they found roughly two-thirds of the errors and corrected them; (⊜) means that they found roughly half of the errors and corrected them. Fewer than half requires a do-over.

Note: Proofreading Triads is the most effective proofreading strategy that I have used and witnessed, but it takes some effort to condition students to work in threes. Introduce the strategy in a fishbowl demonstration using a high-, middle- and low-functioning student. Whatever the method of introduction, the working model of this strategy is the same: groups of three students sit side by side, proofreading each of their three final drafts in turn and writing out the corrections on a proofing strip.

Here is how they helped. Ho Kim called out each word separately, slowly, one word at a time. She called out the capital letters and all of the punctuation. (See page 126, Figure 12.4.) When Ramone or Ho Kim saw a mistake, Ramone corrected it on the proofing strip. I didn't question their choices; I knew they were just suggestions, and I would decide whether to make the changes or not. It was great to see them working so hard on my writing.

When 15 minutes were up, the teacher called time, and Ho Kim and I started finding and correcting the errors on Ramone's final draft. We only had 15 minutes to work, so we got right down to business. Fifteen minutes passes quite fast when you are busy at work. Tape a half sheet of paper to the side of your final draft so the lines match, and you have created a proofing strip. This magical strip will help you and two peers find and fix most of your errors. It is simple.

> **DO**
>
> *Take turns correcting 3/4 of the errors of your PALs on a proofing strip.*

Floyd, Carly and Ahmed proofread Floyd's final draft, sitting side by side, each looking attentively at Floyd's final draft. Like most callers, Carly was eager to find errors in somebody else's writing. Ahmed was eager to fix the mistakes for a (+) in self-assessment. Floyd watched intently to make sure the other two didn't write on his final draft. See what they accomplished in 15 minutes on the first page of Floyd's final draft (page 128, Figure 12.5).

Five errors of the types listed in the Common Core State Standards for fifth grade were not fixed; nineteen errors were: a 79% correction rate. Ahmed led the group in claiming the (+) for performance on one of the three final drafts for proofreading.

Not all triads work as smoothly. I have learned not to be hard-nosed about students staying strictly in their roles, shifting responsibilities with

Figure 12.3 A Proofreading Triad in Action

Writer: Warren	Caller: Ho Kim
	Fixer: Ramone
This past April as a celebration of a wedding anniversary, I drove with my wife, Arnelle, through the Yakima valley of Washington where I spent most of the first thirteen years of my life. Mt. Adams imposed itself from the west. Arnelle's response was immediate, "Now, that's a mountain." We focused on that majestic, dormant, snow-cap volcanoe at each stop on our trip through the lower valley of fruit orchards, vineyards, hop yards and struggling farm towns.	Valley 13 West. snow-capped volcano
	Tape
I was shocked by the size of the house at 703 S. Toppenish Ave. that I called home up through the 3rd grade. I remembered a good-size front lawn that served as a infield diamond for endless games of softball. But now the tiny patches of grass on either side of a short path from sidewalk to porch appeared too small for a lemonade stand, much less fast-paced innings of ball. The boulevard with a tree-lined strip of grass between paved roadways still impressed me, and I pictured long afternoons of hide-and-go-seek and dozens of versions of freeze-tag.	South Avenue third good-sized an ~~But~~ Now two paved freeze tag.

Figure 12.4 Using a Proofing Strip

Ho Kim	[capital T] This past [capital A] April as a celebration of a wedding anniversary, [capital I] I drove with my wife, [capital A] Arnelle, through the [capital Y] Yakima valley of [capital W] Washington where [capital I] I spent most of the first thirteen years of my life. [capital M] Mt. [capital A] Adams imposed itself from the west. [capital A] Arnelle's response was the immediate, "Now, that's a mountain!"
Ramone: Hold it, if Yakima has a capital, then Valley needs one, too. Yakima Valley is a proper name.	
Ho Kim: thirteen is more than ten; it needs numbers.	
Ramone: west is a part of a country. It needs a capital letter.	

the proofreading of each final draft. In some cases, one person dominates the activity regardless of his or her assigned role, and the triad fixes a high percentage of errors in the allotted time. The dynamics of each triad varies. So give students some latitude until you see how productive they are. Conference with unproductive triads as a group to review specific roles.

Once the proofreading is completed, writers transfer corrections to their final drafts. They fold the proofing strip behind the final draft for publishing.

A note about Floyd's final draft: I conferenced with Floyd and six other students who shifted tense in writing a narrative; his draft began in the past tense, but the pirate scene waffled between past and present tense. I made copies of their final drafts so they could change the tense for a skills lesson without affecting their final drafts.

Later, their teacher asked all the students to rewrite a section from a history text in the present tense as a follow up to this proofreading task. The best way to help students understand tense shift is for them to practice it hands-on.

Supporting Student Self-Assessment

The first time you use the Proofreading Triads strategy, help the students assess the degree to which they met expectations. A good target is 3/4 of their errors corrected for each student in the triad. As a student triad completes the first two paragraphs on their own, step up for a brief teacher conference. I always start by asking, "May I help?" How can they refuse?

Read through the first paragraph and write the correction of missed errors in ink on the appropriate line of the proofing strip.

If you have corrected as many errors in ink as the triad corrected in pencil, muse, "Hmm, you found 50% of the errors so far. Let's see—that's a bar (▭) on this writing task? Was that what you were aiming for?"

Every triad that heard me ask this question immediately understood my point, and I hear, "Oh, we weren't finished yet; we were going back over that part." Of course, they weren't, but moving forward, they proceeded more carefully, holding one another more responsible for finding and correcting the errors.

Most triads catch on quickly when you hold them accountable for finding and correcting their own errors. The students quickly learn that the standard for proofreading is a group responsibility—15 minutes for correcting errors in each paper. What their triad doesn't fix, students must fix by themselves. Their brains alert them to get busy, and once they succeed at correcting errors, proofreading becomes a task that they look forward to in the next Writing Cycle.

Let students place the +, ◎ or ▭ at the top of each proofing strip and in the self-check column of the Writing Cycle Log for Student Self-Check.

Figure 12.5 A Proofreading Triad in Action

Exciting Trip to Las Vegas	Caller: Carly
Floyd Gruber	Fixer: Ahmed
The Delta Plane took 4 hours to get to Las Vegas. Then the lucky Gruber family went to get our rental car to go to our hotel. I took us forever to get the car but when we did we were gone to the city.	Delta plane four I → It car, but
After we left the airport we had to go passed a lot of hotels. We saw many sites and hotels before we got to our Hotel. The first one we passed was a hotel in a Egyptian monument. After awhile there were just plane hotels but on the side of the road there were many things. My personal favorite was the mini-volcano. It was defineately the best road site. When we stepped out of our car, my dad was sure glad he was wearing a Big Black overcoat and warm leather gloves. The Strip was like a wind tunnel. Later that night, we walked the strip and came to Treasure Island casino first. One of the nicest hotels in Vegas. We watched the pirates fight in the scene at the hotel. The whole drama took place outside of the hotel lobby at Treasure Island. It started off with a big ship sailing towards another ship. Then it stops and a lot of pirates start to shot at the other ship. Soon cannons start to fire on the other ship and there are little explosions on the first ship. Then first ship shoots cannons of there own and it sinks the other ship. The pirates start to cheer while the other ship is still sinking. There pirates are jumping overboard. Then the lights go dark and it is all over. As we walked away I pulled my Michigan sweatshirt down over my Nylon pants to stay warm.	passed → past hotel an Egyptian plain hotels, but definitely big black , one shoot , and the their , and Their , and nylon

Review their work and estimate the degree of accuracy in their assessment. There is no doubt, proofreading sessions are the most exciting example of students working harder than their teachers. So relax in later proofreading sessions, and let them work. Have some fun by inserting your final draft (with attached proofing strip) into one of the triads, and proofread with two students in need of your attention.

> **Caveat:** Use rough estimates for scoring student performance in proofreading triads. Do not get caught up calculating the percent of errors down to the hundredths. Hold students firmly accountable, but be generous when you see students collaborating with obvious, engaged effort. Many teachers say that proofreading is the high point of the writing process for their classes. It is exciting to see students succeed in a writing task that many parents, administrators and students notice first in final drafts on display.

```
┌─────────────────┐
│     LOOK        │
│  Transfer       │
│  the useful     │
│  corrections    │
│  from the       │
│  Proofing Strip │
│  to your final  │
│  draft.         │
└─────────────────┘
```

On a page from a flip chart that can be affixed to the wall, lead the students in reflecting on their proofreading routine. They may come up with observations like the following from a class of fourth-graders.

"Fixing errors is easy to do with two helpers."
"Most errors are little mistakes."
"It's hard to find your own errors."
"You don't need a dictionary to fix most errors."

What does proofreading mean? At some point after students have learned to proofread *by* proofreading, you may choose to help students dissect *proofreading* and understand it its component parts.

> ### Defining Proofreading
>
> Simplistic notions of proofreading are so deeply embedded in the thinking of some students that you simply need to redefine *proofreading* directly. *Proofreading* has three parts to its definition.
>
> - *Proof-* means "test" or "trial." Read final drafts word-for-word and punctuation-for-punctuation with great care.
>
> - *-read-* means "to understand, study, infer and interpret." *Proofread*, then, is very slow reading.
>
> - *-ing* means "the act of," reminding us that proofreading is a separate, distinct act in the writing process. Students need to hear this definition from each of their writing teachers.

Proofreading occurs prior to the final draft only on special occasions (such as a large number of errors). For the most efficient use of class time, proofreading of final drafts should take place only during in-class time on week 5 of a Writing Cycle.

After practicing proofreading strategies in this chapter, your students will be ready to talk about proofreading in new and productive ways (Combs, 2011).

Since proofreading with such concrete, specific strategies engages students, they are ready to draw conclusions about their engaged practice. Listen to each comment carefully and record what you hear. Fifth-graders whom I recently met concluded:

"Some readers really get upset by our errors."

"Proofreading isn't really reading; it's just calling out words real slow."

"Fixers aren't bosses; we don't have to do what they write."

"Fixing errors takes three people."

"Proofing strips make proofreading easy."

"I'm glad nobody can write on my final draft."

"We surprised Ms. Rainey with all our corrections."

The list of conclusions from your classes will vary from this list, but the lessons learned should focus on the proofreading practices presented here.

Extending Practice with Proofreading

Move students toward correcting errors on their own with a Sentence Check Chart for Proofreading. Read the student exemplar on page 131 and download a blank to print out for your students at www.eyeoneducation.com. Teachers use the chart for different purposes. I placed students in PALS to work on a first draft that they chose not to revise. In essence, that first draft became a conventions worksheet.

- Each PAL numbers the first sixteen sentences in his final draft.
- The PALs work together to list the errors to be corrected in the Error column of each of their charts.
- Then the PALs continue working on their own papers, inserting corrections in the fourth column and combining or dividing sentences to ensure a variety of sentence lengths in the fifth column.

Figure 12.6 Sentence Check Chart

NO.	FIRST WORD	ERROR	CORRECTION	# OF WORDS	NOTES
1	Well	Well / figered	Well, figured	9	
2	I'm	I'm / assome	I'm assume	10	
3	You	exieding x 2	exciting x 2	14	
4	Wait	Wait / exieding	Wait, exciting	5	
5	So	So	So,	5	
6	Alligators	Alligators / paravnas / chose	Alligators piranhas choose	15	
7	Both	exspencive / there	expensive their	7	
8	But	There	their	8	
9	So	Probly	probably	9	
10	That	don't / to	don't too	10	
11	O	O don't vejes there	Oh, don't veggies. They're	10	
12	Know	suplies / rember / theres	supplies remember there's	10	
13	That	Plural	plural	3	
14	If	don't / plueral	don't plural	12	
15					
16					

In Ms. Knight's class, Caleb and Chanteau tackled one of Caleb's first drafts with the following result. Note how apparent Caleb's error profile became in just fourteen sentences: his issues are with spelling, apostrophes and commas; he has no problems with capitalization or end punctuation. Ms. Knight made note of Caleb's strengths so she could PAL him with a person who could use his help in the next proofreading session.

Additional proofreading strategies of equal intention and concrete expectations appear in the section on proofreading in *A Writing Cycle for Writer's Workshop*, pp. P-10–PR-17.

A Final Comment

Many students are amazed that their teachers' and my final drafts need proofreading. After students find and correct errors on my final draft, they offer without being asked.

> "Don't you ever write perfect papers?"
> "Do your mistakes make you mad, too?"
> "You're just making mistakes so we don't feel bad."
> "Who finds your mistakes when you write at home?"
> "I didn't think real authors made mistakes."

Their comments and questions reminded me why I keep joining groups of Proofreading Triads. When I offer up a copy of my final draft to the devices of students, they acquire critical insights into writing that can be learned no other way. Like other members of my Proofreading Triad, I was ready to take my turn in the author's chair before me and feel published.

Some thoughts on proofreading final drafts

The days of teachers correcting student errors should be over; students experience success by finding their own errors. But avoid letting students exchange papers to look for each other's errors independently. Trading papers to proofread has posted a dismal track record.

- Students proofread only final drafts. Proofreading earlier drafts spawn drafts that contain new mistakes to be corrected.

- Students always proofread in groups—usually in twos or threes, although other configurations can achieve the goal of student-led proofreading.

- Students always use a proofing strip attached to their final drafts so that all errors are noted and corrected off of the actual final draft. Completed strips remain folded behind the first draft for later inspection.

- Teachers set specific expectations and model the error types and percent of errors fixed.

- Students realize that corrections made by peers are to be considered seriously, but they are not required corrections.

- On the computer, peers use the "Track Changes" function for correcting errors, and writers use the "Accept" or "Reject" option for each correction.

Looking Back

In your response journal, discuss the pros and cons of proofreading final drafts yourself or letting peers do the work. Were you surprised that students found errors in your own final draft? In a second entry, discuss the value of using an author's chair for sharing progress in proofreading in a class you currently teach.

Looking Ahead

What opportunities coming up in your curriculum invite you to use a proofing strip to assist students in proofreading their final drafts?

Chapter 13

Score a Final Draft with Me

Common Core State Standards for Speaking and Listening
Comprehension and Collaboration—1. Prepare for and participate effectively in a range of conversations and collaborations building on others' ideas and expressing their own clearly and persuasively.

"Do not bother just to be better than others.
Try to be better than yourself."

—Willam Faulkner

In traditional grading, a final grade is all that enters the grade book. In a Writing Cycle, scores of three first drafts, a revision task, a proofreading task and a final evaluation appear as formative assessment. A Final Evaluation Rubric simply brings all of the fruitful work of the Writing Cycle to a close. It returns students to the big picture of the writing process—the standard of a writing genre.

It is a joy to see students take the final evaluation score of a Writing Cycle in stride, treating it as only one of six parts of their overall performance in writing. The Writing Cycle puts the score of a final draft in proper perspective. It celebrates the accumulative efforts of the steps that came before it. It provides incentive for students to remain fully engaged in the writing process up to the end. Full engagement in all six writing tasks from start to finish is what teaching and learning to write is all about. It's time to bring closure to the successes and struggles of a Writing Cycle.

A deeper presence of assessment and evaluation in writing
Effective teachers of the writing process allow students to self-assess their performance and evaluate their progress at specific times throughout the process. Just like they self-assessed their prewriting and drafting tasks, students will self-evaluate their final drafts.

- My Assignment Page and word bank required students to assess their performance on prewriting as individuals or PALs.

- In their first drafts, students self-assessed the degree to which they met their teachers' expectations and their faithfulness to their word bank.

- In revision, students peer-assessed at least one other student's use of a prompted revision strategy. They judged whether the revision fit the draft and whether it was too much, too little or just the right amount of revision.

- In proofreading, students self-assessed the collaborative work with their PALs.

- In this chapter, students complete the Final Evaluation Rubric in pencil before their teachers score it in pen.

Additionally, at the close of the daily work sessions in the author's chair, students shared their writing with PALs and recorded their response. Each week, they compared their self-assessment on the Writing Cycle Log for Student Self-Check with the points that their teachers awarded. Over time, they saw their self-assessment move closer to that of their teacher's assessment. In other words, the assessment and evaluation of writing is much more than scoring the final product of the writing process. They are the engines that help students self-power the work sessions of each writing task.

Invite your students to evaluate their final drafts—to recognize and value the traits of effective writing. A Final Evaluation Rubric is a remarkable instructional tool when the rubric is at once student-friendly, true to stated standards and instructive for students. Most rubrics published commercially on the Internet fit one or maybe two of these criteria, but none fit all three; it took years of testing and modifying rubrics to produce ones that satisfied all three criteria. We started with the adopted state rubrics in Georgia, South Carolina and South Dakota, along with the 6+1 Trait Writing rubric. Then we created a rubric in the mode of every word bank. Over a period of several years, students used up to fifteen Final Evaluation Rubrics, from character sketch to research summaries. (See www.writingtowin.com for the ones used in this book, and *The Writing Cycle for Writer's Workshop* for all fifteen [Combs, 2011, pp. E-18–E-32].) How gratifying it was to see students assess their final drafts with ease. We worked hard to keep them true to stated standards of writing for students. Student performance data suggests that we did just that.

The first time students evaluate final drafts with you, ask "Why do you think I say that we *evaluate* our final drafts instead of grade them?" If most students have no confident or accurate response, help the class with a follow-up question: "What little word do you see inside of *evaluate*?" Some of them say *value*—and that word makes all the difference in how they look at each other's final drafts. They are looking for what is of value, what is strong—exactly what they have been focusing on throughout the Writing Cycle. It is no wonder that students embrace the Final Evaluation Rubrics of a Writing Cycle with chatty, productive energy.

Lesson with Scripting for Final Evaluation Rubrics

> **INVITE**
>
> *Score a final draft with me.*

Teacher: **Evaluate final drafts with me.** It is time for us to bring this Writing Cycle to a close with a Final Evaluation Rubric. Rubrics help us describe in words the value in the writing that we read. First we will score a final draft together—working through it one trait of writing at a time. This helps us identify evidence of the trait and agree on the score for it. The total score tells writers exactly how close their writing is to the stated standard. It is that simple, so let's get started. Score your final draft along with me.

> **MODEL**
>
> *Review a completed Final Evaluation Rubric on a final draft of a previous topic.*

Since we wrote our final drafts in the narrative genre, we use a Final Evaluation Rubric for Narration. The rubric contains language that helps us talk about the traits of narrative writing. It is easy to use and understand. We call it formative assessment. As you use the rubric, it will help you form an understanding of what makes up good writing. Your teacher and I will use the same rubric, too, when we place a final score on your final drafts. Thanks to the rubric, we teachers join the conversation with you about your final draft.

Notice how different this rubric is from the First Draft Response Form that focused on only one trait of writing—the development of your main idea. Final Evaluation Rubrics often respond to as many as six traits of writing at a time. When you add up the value of the assessment of each trait, you arrive at a final grade that goes into the grade book. Notice the Final Evaluation Rubric for Narration on page 21 of your Working Portfolios (page 140 of this chapter).

Read through the Final Evaluation Rubric with me. Someone read the first line aloud. The rest of us will circle the key words in each of the three comments as we hear them read.

[After the reading] Someone tell us what words you circled in the left comment.

Figure 13.1 Circling Key Words

Voice (Vocabulary)					
1	2	3	4	5	x 4 pts =

You seem to use (only words you can spell.) Good. You use (some words) to (help me) (see your thoughts) and feelings. Your words show me (a clear description) (of your thoughts) and feelings.

Student:	"Only words you can spell."
Teacher:	Good, when we use only words we can spell, we muffle our writing voices or style. Someone tell us what you circled in the middle comment.
Student:	"Some words help me see your thoughts."
Teacher:	Some words, but not all the words that are needed for me to see vivid pictures of your thoughts and ideas. More vivid words are needed. What words did someone circle in the right comment?
Student:	"I circled 'a clear description of your thoughts.'"
Teacher:	Nice, will someone remind us of the difference between words that show us and words that tell?
Student:	"*Telling* words just give bare facts without details. *Showing* words help us see the pictures that are in the writer's mind."

The discussion of the rubric continues in like manner until the dimensions of each trait have been explained orally by members of the class. When the rubric is fully explored, the students are ready to apply it to the writing of one of their peers who agrees to let the class score their writing.

Enjoy this snapshot of Ms. Wilks' and Ms. McNeirney's upper elementary class at Swannanoa Valley Montessori School, North Carolina. Isaiah volunteered on a day I visited his class. His final draft follows. The bold font marks his revision using the Circling Picture Sentences revision strategy.* Ms. Wilks projected his final draft on the screen as he read. His peers all had the Final Evaluation Rubric for Narration in front of them to mark immediately after he finished reading.

When I was three I really wanted to play teeball, so my mom signed me up for the next season. The next year I had my first practice and the best thing about it was that it was at night. To me it was good because I could stay up till like 10 o'clock, but to my mom it was bad because she knew I would be grumpy in the morning. This wouldn't be the first time.

I had an advantage because my mom was the coach. We didn't have to wery about getting to practice because the field that we were going to was walking distance from our house. When we got there all we had to do was wait. All the rest of the kids and the parents got there only to turn into a disaster. **It looked like a toddler civil war.** I was the only 4-year-old that wasn't running around like a menace. **Brothers beating each other up, one kid sitting on mothers face and eight kids having a 4-way boxing match. I really was the only one being normal.**

Finally when all the kids were caught we got in positions. The catcher was this short guy with really long hair, 1st base was this fat kid with a buz cut, 2nd base was me, 3rd base was my friend Dillon who was just an all around guy. My mom decided all the parents would just run around the bases and not hit the ball which I thought was the stupidest idea ever, but I went with it anyway. My mom ran last but she actually hit the ball it went like a meteor really high (It was probably only 5 ft high, but I couldn't tell. I was like 3 feet tall myself).

You know what? The **crazy** ball came right to me, and I got my first catch. **I was so happy I was jumping like crazy,** I yelled to Dillon's dad Dave, "I caught it!!" **He gave me a short laughy smile and looked away. That look got to me, so I got this really serious look back at him. I threw the ball as fast as I could to Dillon, and he caught. He started racing his dad to the base and he beat him.** What a close call! ~~I threw the ball as fast as I could to Dillon who was on third. He caught it and got his dad out.~~ I was so happy because I pulled in my first catch, and I made my first double play.

*Circling Picture Sentences prompts students to circle four or five sentences in their first draft that make a clear picture return to their minds. They select the two circled sentences that they could write the even more about and add four or more sentences to each. Students often rewrite the circled sentence in their revision like Isaiah did in his last revision. Since Isaiah wrote more about three circled sentences, he exceeded Ms. Wilks' expectation and earned a +.

Ms. Wilks [darkening the image of Isaiah's projected final draft]: Thanks, Isaiah. I'll take the lead as each of us scores Isaiah's writing. Then we'll put out ideas together to share with Isaiah. We just met the rubric for narration. It's time now to circle a comment on the first three traits of the rubric without looking at Isaiah's writing. [The full rubric is shown in Figure 13.3, page 140.]

Trait #1: voice. Did Isaiah's story make you feel and see his thoughts about his first T-ball game? Circle the left, middle or right comment that you think describes his writing.

Trait #2: pictures of people. Did Isaiah's writing help you picture the people in his story? Circle the left, middle or right comment that you think fits his writing.

Trait #3: pictures of places. Did Isaiah's writing paint a picture of the place where the game took place? Circle the left, middle or right comment that you think fits his writing.

Ms. Wilks: I'm projecting Isaiah's final draft again. Read it over quickly and circle the comments that best describe the last three traits of Isaiah's writing: the beginning, the ending and proofreading. Take 2 minutes.

[Two minutes later] Now take another minute to circle a number on each trait that goes with the comment you circled. For example, if you circled the comment on the left, you must circle either the *1* or *2* just above the comment. You cannot circle anything higher than a 2 even if you don't want to hurt Isaiah's feelings. When you circle the middle comment, you may circle a *2*, *3* or *4*. Got it? When you circle the right comment, you must circle either a *4* or *5*. Give it a try. You can do it.

[One minute later] Nice work. Now we'll move to the last step. I'll ask four of you to read the six numbers that you circled.

Rachel's hand went up first, so Ms. Wilks chose her. Rachel's numbers are in the first row below.

Figure 13.2 Student Responses

Student	Voice	People	Places	Beginning	Ending	Proofing
Rachel	5	4	2	4	5	3
Ellie	4	3	1	3	4	2
Caleb	5	5	3	5	5	3
Sadie	4	4	3	4	4	4
Consensus	5	4	2	4	5	3

The class agreed that Isaiah exceeded expectations on voice, people, beginning and ending. "The voice was the strongest trait," quipped Rachel. "Yet I could picture the 'fat kid with the buzz cut,'" said another. "His final sentence sums up the whole story. Who wouldn't be happy with a double play?" asked Caleb.

He approached the standard on places and met the standard on proofreading. Carrie said, "I couldn't picture the setting of the T-ball game at all; was it like a field or a stadium? Who can tell?" Isaiah spoke up as he

Figure 13.3   Rubric for Narration

Narration

WRITER _____ EVALUATOR _____

Circle one comment and the corresponding number in each row that best tells how you respond to that trait of writing in a draft of a fellow writer. Multiply the circled number by the point value listed at the end of the row, and place the product in the margin at the right. For the total raw score, add the numbers in the right-hand margin. Convert the total raw score, using page 142. Comments on this form are a guide. Change any comments to represent your evaluation more accurately.

Voice (Vocabulary)

1	2	3	4	5	x 4 pts =
You seem to use only words you can spell.		Good. You use some words to help me see your thoughts and feelings.		Your words show me a clear description of your thoughts and feelings.	

The People in Your Narration

1	2	3	4	5	x 3 pts =
Which people in this event do you recall?		You mention the people in the event. Add words that show me more about them.		Your words help me see a picture of the people in the event.	

The Places in Your Narration

1	2	3	4	5	x 3 pts =
In what place did the event happen? I cannot tell by reading your words.		You tell me the place(s) in the event. Add words that show me more about them.		The words you use help me see the places where the event happened.	

The Beginning

1	2	3	4	5	x 3 pts =
You start writing somewhere in the middle of the event.		You start writing about the beginning, but write more.		Your first words show me exactly how the event began.	

Ending

1	2	3	4	5	x 3 pts =
Your writing stops before it gets to the end of the event.		Your writing reaches the end of the event. Write more about it.		The ending of your draft helps me see how the event ended.	

Proofreading

1	2	3	4	5	x 4 pts =
Your errors make your draft hard to read and understand.		Your errors are few but easy to see; be more careful.		It was tough to find any errors at all. Bravo!	

Converted Score: _____   **Total Raw Score:** _____

wrote a note in the margin of his paper. "It was at the parks and recreation field in Virginia Beach."

Caleb chimed in with a positive comment for his buddy: "You said if we could read his paper without slowing down, he gets a 3 on proofreading. I didn't slow down a bit." It was gratifying to hear students talk about their writing with one another so easily and productively. The full rubric is shown on page 140.

Evaluating a Final Draft (Persuasive Genre)

> **DO**
>
> *Complete a Final Evaluation Rubric on a peer's final draft.*

Teacher: Read completely through your final draft before you start marking the Final Evaluation Rubric for Support an Opinion (see page 146). Then, without looking back at the draft, circle the comments on the first three traits (voice, word pictures and support) that fit your opinion of each. Once you have circled the comments, select a corresponding number from 1 to 5. If you circled the left comment, circle the number 1 or 2. If you circled the middle comment, circle a 2, 3 or 4. Circle the numbers 4 or 5 when you circle the right comment.

Reread your final draft quickly to score the ending and proofreading. Finally, score your paper for its overall effect. Do you think your writing will convince readers of your opinion? Be ready to defend all six of your choices on this rubric.

When you have scored all six traits on the Support an Opinion rubric, compute the total score. Multiply the number you circled for each trait by the multiplier to the right and place the "weighted score" in the right margin. Then add up the scores for each trait and place the sum in the box labeled "total score." Use the conversion chart on page 142 to convert the total score to one that fits in a 70- to 100-point grading scale.

Note: Even though a Final Evaluation Rubric is a standards-based tool, *Writer's Workshop for the Common Core* continues to correlate the raw score of the rubric to traditional grading scales of 70 to 100 points or A through F. This is an attempt to bridge the gap between the standards-based instruction of teachers and traditional perceptions of grading of students and their parents.

Scoring Final Drafts after Peer Evaluation

Listen in on Ms. Brewer's class as she addressed her fifth-grade students at Ringgold Elementary in north Georgia. Previously, she asked

Figure 13.4 Conversion Chart
(for converting a total score to a 70-point scale)

If the total score is:	The converted score is:	If the total score is:	The converted score is:
98	99	58	79
96	98	56	78
94	97	54	77
92	96	52	76
90	95	50	75
88	94	48	74
86	93	46	73
84	92	44	72
82	91	42	71
80	90	40	70
78	89	38	69
76	88	36	68
74	87	34	67
72	86	32	66
70	85	30	65
68	84	28	64
66	83	26	63
64	82	24	62
62	81	22	61
60	80	20	60

students to self-evaluate their final drafts in pencil using a Final Evaluation Rubric for narrative (first quarter) and expository writing (second quarter). She found that students tended to underevaluate themselves before handing in their scored final drafts for her evaluation. In the third quarter, her students completed a persuasive Writing Cycle. For this cycle, she allowed PALs to peer-evaluate one another's final drafts. She felt that the persuasive genre called for peer-evaluation since persuasion seeks a stronger impact on an audience. The rest of the final evaluation routine remained the same. Just as with narrative and informational genre, she led a classroom discussion through the traits of the standards of persuasive genre. She based the discussion on a student draft that she read and knew met the standard of the genre on this writing topic prompt.

This time she asked Morgan to let the class view her final draft and see if the class agreed with her PAL Callie's evaluation. Morgan gladly hopped into the author's chair and read her final draft, which was projected on the interactive board behind her. Her twenty-four classmates each had a copy of the Final Evaluation Rubric for Support an Opinion for scoring Morgan's draft after she read it. They sat with pencils on their desk in rapt attention.

The following conversation that ensued was instructive for teachers and students alike. The students were all fond of the writer, Morgan, and the nominee, Pressley Ann. They knew that they were strong-performing students in every subject, so it was hard for them to score this paper below a 3 on any trait. Yet before our very eyes, that is exactly what happened. What a learning experience for those fifth-graders! A paper could score a 2 on one trait and still meet—and even exceed—the standard overall!

Dear Mrs. Erwin,

Presley Ann has been my friend since first grade when I moved here. She was my first friend and she was the only one who was ever nice to me. Also, she still is one of my best friends ever. She is a really good friend, actually, a good friend with everyone. I think she should be on the wall of fame.

Do you have a best friend? Well, I do. My best friend is Presley Ann. She will make you happy if you're sad. She is the best friend a girl could have. She is so sweet and kind.

One time our teacher said to put our work away, and she kept on working all the way through recess. When the class came back inside, she was working on another paper! I'm telling you, if you put her on the wall of fame, you will not regret it. She is a really hard, hard worker. She loves to work every day.

Presley Ann has a good attitude. Even when someone of the environment is negative she is positive. She is always up beat. That's what I like about her. She is helpful, she will help anyone do anything. She is so nice, she is my best friend.

Thank you for reading this Mrs. Erwin. Have a good day. I think Presley Ann should be on the wall of fame because she is a good friend, has a good attitude, is helpful, and is a hard worker. All fifth graders will be proud to see her picture on the wall of fame.

Yours truly,
Morgan B.

See Figure 13.5 (page 146) for the scored rubric for Morgan. You can see that her peer Callie was like many beginning evaluators. She didn't separate her friendship with the writer from her evaluation of the writing. After that class discussion, Callie explained her high evaluation of Morgan's writing. "Morgan's a good writer. She's sure better than me." Over time, Callie—and all beginning evaluators—start to let the rubric do more of the evaluating and leave less of the responsibility to opinion.

To sum up each trait of the discussion:

- **Voice:** The class scored her paper lower (3) on voice than Callie (4). "The vocabulary was okay," said one student. Another quipped, "Actually, a lot of Morgan's words are on the Picture Killers chart—*sweet, nice, kind, really, good.*" Still another, "Yeah, her writing wasn't as fun as the way she talks." The class did agree that Morgan's voice presented strong emotion.
- **Word Pictures of Your Opinion:** The class gave the paper a 3, while Callie scored it another 4. "I didn't see all of the pictures in her writing. I saw Presley working during recess. That was all. I mean, the opinion was really strong. It just didn't have really clear pictures." [The writing supports the peer's point.]
- **Support:** This one took just a few minutes for the class to process. First, the class seemed to stick with the 3 for meeting standard. Then a voice exclaimed, "It gets a 2 because it just *tells* the reasons. She didn't tell a story to go with any of the reasons but one. You have to have a story for each reason to get a 3."

This last student really let the rubric do the scoring. Typically, students who take a risk like this are the only students in the class who give a good student a 2. Fortunately for Ms. Brewer's class, that's all it took. He convinced the class that he was right; even Morgan saw his point.

Everyone seemed happy, especially Ms. Brewer and me. Although this was a remarkable discovery for Ms. Brewer's class, I see the final evaluation rubrics prompt learning like this again and again. This is the kind of learning that years of direct teacher talk seldom produce.

Wisely, Ms. Brewer stepped up to this teachable moment. Giving "the support" a 2 means only that this was the least valuable trait in Morgan's paper. "You wait and see; her writing may still meet the standard overall. Many papers that meet standard will have one trait that is scored lower than the other five."

- Everyone agreed with Callie on the traits of ending and proofreading, awarding each a 4.
- The class differed from Callie again on the last trait, the overall comment. It scored the paper a 3 instead of a 5 because a 3 was now the average of the first five traits. Callie's 5 was more than likely a friendly gesture, and Ms. Brewer didn't mind. She knew that it took time for students to shift from peer-evaluation that dispensed personal feelings to peer-evaluation that identified evidence of a standard in the writing.

What a satisfying conclusion, and what an important lesson learned. Because the lesson required practice by doing (see the average retention rates in chapter 1, page 9), students will retain what they learned much longer than if the teacher had taught the lesson directly. Students scoring student's writing provides clear evidence that teachers practice the philosophy of "Talk less, write more."

Ms. Brewer truly understands the importance of final evaluation rubrics in scoring her students' final drafts. She reports that it takes her about 3 minutes to read through each student's final draft and score the rubric in ink. That's 75 minutes to score all twenty-five papers! In one of her three sections of students, ten of the twenty-five peer-assessed final drafts were scored to her satisfaction. She was elated, and so was I. She celebrated the short time it took her to read the ten drafts, review the ten scored rubrics and write "I agree with your assessment." Why shouldn't she? It took less than 2 minutes per paper. More importantly, she and I celebrated the student evidence of acquired understanding of the standard of persuasive writing.

Scoring Final Drafts after Peer Evaluation

Of course, Ms. Brewer had reason to celebrate. Yet the majority of her students scored their writing and that of their peers differently than she did. To put it bluntly, she concluded that ten out of twenty-five students scoring the standard accurately is a good bit better than was any previous year. She's not alone in this experience. Most teachers I have met, even the

Figure 13.5   Rubric for an Opinion/Solution

Support an Opinion/Solution

WRITER ___Morgan B.___ EVALUATOR ___Callie D.___

Circle one comment and the corresponding number in each row that best tells how you respond to that writing trait in the draft of a fellow writer. Multiply the circled number by the point value listed at the end of the row, and place the product in the margin at the right. For the total raw score, add the numbers in the right-hand margin. Convert the total raw score using page 142. Comments on this form are a guide. Change any comments to represent your evaluation more accurately.

Voice (Vocabulary)

1	2	(3)	4	5	x 3 pts =
You are using only words that you can spell. Use the best words in your mind.		Some good words, but add the extra words that are in your mind.		Your words let me know exactly how you really think.	

Word Pictures of Your Opinion

1	2	(3)	4	5	x 4 pts =
What opinion/solution are you describing? I cannot see it in my mind.		I can see some pictures coming to my mind. Help me see more details.		I see clear pictures of your opinon/solution in my mind. Nice job!	

The Support

1	(2)	3	4	5	x 5 pts =
The rest of your paper does not explain why you hold your opinion/solution.		You tell me reasons for your opinion/solution. Tell me a little story about each of them.		You show me a clear picture of each reason. Strong and full support.	

Ending

1	2	3	(4)	5	x 3 pts =
No ending. It just quits.		Ending is adequate, but not convincing.		A convincing conclusion.	

Proofreading

1	2	3	(4)	5	x 2 pts =
Your errors make your draft hard to read and understand.		A few obvious errors that do not harm your meaning.		It was tough to find any errors at all. Nice!	

Overall Comments

1	2	(3)	4	5	x 3 pts =
Picture your opinion/solution and reasons before you write!		Use more words that show me what you mean.		A complete and enjoyable draft.	

Converted Score: 80   **Total Raw Score:** 60

master teachers of writer's workshop, feel confident that their students understand the standards they teach. I understand completely how they feel. I used to feel that way. Yet until they have student-scored rubrics in their hands, they have no data. Australian educator Derek Wenmoth challenges us: "Without data, you are just another person with an opinion" (Derek's blog, April 23, 2009). In previous years, Ms. Brewer felt many of her students understood the standards she was teaching. Now she knows, and to her and to me as well, knowing makes all the difference.

It seems normal for students to undervalue their writing at first. I found an example of this an eighth-grade class at Heritage Middle School, Georgia. Carl took the author's chair and explained what a positive impact his grandparents made on him. Here are Carl's first paragraphs:

> Have you ever met someone who you know is an amazing person right when you see them? If you have have, you probably saw my grandparents. The two of them are one of the best things in my life, and I love them so much. I wouldn't trade them fare anything. Whenever they pass away, hopefully never, I will remember them the most for fantastic food, sleeping in the pool and taking pictures.
>
> My grandma, (whom we call Gran), is the most loving and caring person in the world. One of her best qualitys is that she loves to prepare food. My family goes over to my cousin's house all the time, and every time we're there, she fixes a feast. We get to pig ourselves out of a seven or eight course meal. She also fixes food for her church. She goes to a fairly large church in Chickimaga, and she cooks for just about everyone there once a week. She is constantly preparing food and she loves it.
>
> My grandfather, (whom we call Papaw), is one of the best Papaws ever. When he is gone, there will be one thing about him that will stand out above the rest of the memories. That is, sleeping on the pool float. Every time that we gather at my cousin's pool, Papaw gets there early, grabs the pool float and his straw hat, and falls asleep. He floats were ever the water takes him. Lying on his back, hat over eyes, hands meshed together on his stomach, its really a sight to see.

Carl consistently scored himself lower than his teacher did on four of the six traits of writing. (See Figure 13.6.) He and Ms. Newsome agreed on one

Figure 13.6   Carl's Final Rubric

WRITER _____ Carl H. _____   EVALUATOR _____ Ms. Newsome _____

Circle one comment and corresponding number in each row that best tells how you respond to that trait of writing in a draft of a fellow writer. Multiply the circled number by the point value listed at the end of the row, and place the product in the margin at the right. For the total raw score, add the numbers in the right-hand margin. Convert the total raw score, using page 142. Comments on this form are a guide. Change any comments to represent your evaluation more accurately.

Voice (Vocabulary)

1	2	3	(4)	5	x 4 pts =
You seem to use only words that you can spell.		Good. You spell some descriptive words the best that you can.		Your words show me a lot about the character(s).	

Outside Features of Your Character

1	2	3	4	(5)	x 3 pts =
Show me what your character looks like on the outside.		Good. I begin to see some outside features. Show me more.		Your words help me picture your character in my mind.	

Inside Features of Your Character

1	2	(3)	4	5	x 3 pts =
Your words do not tell me about your character's likes, personality or emotions.		Your words tell me about your character's inside features. Show me how he or she acts.		You show me the inside features of your character in the behaviors that you describe.	

Beginning

1	2	3	(4)	5	x 3 pts =
You start writing without telling about some basic features of your character.		You mention some important details from the start. Add even more of them.		Your beginning words start painting a picture of your character in my mind.	

Ending

1	(2)	3	4	5	x 3 pts =
Your draft stops before I see your character at all.		Your draft stops before I see your character fully.		Your ending gives me full and final details.	

Proofreading

1	2	3	(4)	5	x 4 pts =
Errors prevent me from understanding your meaning.		Errors interrupt the flow of meaning in your first draft.		I had to look hard to find any errors in your draft.	

Translated Score [87]   **Total Raw Score** [74]

(internal features), and he scored himself higher than she did on his lead paragraph. All in all, Carl gave his final draft a raw score of 60 and a converted score of 80. Ms. Newsome scored it a 74 and 87, respectively, a difference between posting Carl's final draft on the classroom wall under the heading "Approaching Standard" (Carl) and "Meets Standard" (Ms. Newsome).

Students typically undervalue their final drafts at first.

| Trait | Score | | | Explanation |
	Carl	Ms. Newsome	Weight	
Voice	3	4	x 4	16—Don't hesitate to use better words that are hard to spell!
External features	4	5	x 3	15—Graphic word pictures of your granddad and the famous feast your grams prepares.
Internal features	3	3	x 3	9—Help me with which internal feature your examples imply, like is Papaw self-absorbed or playfully competitive?
Beginning	3	4	x 3	12—Clear and concise, but not engaging.
Ending	3	2	x 3	6—Short and heartfelt, but I still don't understand the positive impact you feel from your grandparents.
Proofreading	2	4	x 4	20—Your handwriting is not neat, but I had to hunt for errors.

Raw score   74

Converted score   87 = meets the standard

Students Scoring the Standard with Accuracy

With increasing frequency, your students shift to scoring their final drafts more like you. Read and enjoy Dawson's attempt to persuade Ms. Brewer's class to vote for his ultimate field trip. Although this final draft was written in the same Writing Cycle as Morgan's, Dawson selected his 1st Draft #2, written in his social studies class, to take to publication. The impact of Ms. Brewer's team planning with social studies team member Mr. Giannamore is unmistakable. It is precisely the direction that the Common Core State Standards are prompting us teachers to take.

> Did you know that artifacts of Vikings, such as swords, shields and even Viking bones, have been found in Iceland? It's covered in green grass along most of the island even though

it's called Iceland. It was named that to trick settlers seeking for new land. There are waterfalls, rocks you could climb and more. Do you think Ms. Brewer's class should go there? How long? Well, I think that we should go there, say, for five days.

Not only is it fun; it's educational too. You could learn about the island's history. I know this is a little bit off topic, but I want to tell you anyway. Greenland is covered in ice and Iceland is covered in grass. Now that's some interesting trivia. Let's get back on topic now. From looking at pictures I can see that Iceland's an awesome and fun looking place. Now it's time for me to see for myself—and you can come, too.

Old weaponry was found there like swords, axes, daggers, shields and such. Archeologist found the weapons with the bones of Vikings. The weapons were completely dull (not sharp). The weapons could help teach us about the history of the island. Could they really be the weapons of the Viking? That's something that we could find out there when we visited.

Vikings bones were found there too. Some of them were buried with their weapons. Not just any Viking that lived there was buried with their weapons. Not just any Viking that lived there was buried in the ground. Only the Vikings who died there after doing something heroic were buried there—and, of course, the ones who owned a lot of land. The Viking bones could also teach about the island's history. What else is waiting to be found there? When we go we'll find out.

Iceland sounds like somewhere we should visit for sure. Well, that's what I think. What about you? That's what I know about it. That's why I think we should go to Iceland.

Dawson and Ms. Brewer scored his final draft a 5 on voice (vocabulary), word pictures of your opinion and the support and overall comment. Dawson scored his ending a 5, while Ms. Brewer scored it a 3. He gave himself a 3 for proofreading because his handwriting "stinks." Ms. Brewer scored it a 4, reminding him that handwriting isn't all there is to proofreading. His score for overall comments was a 4; Ms. Brewer's score was a 5. Although Ms. Brewer and Dawson varied on three traits, their total scores matched. In the final evaluation conference, it was obvious that his sense of the standard was well conceived.

<table>
<tr><td>

LOOK

Assess your use of a Final Evaluation Rubric on your final draft.

</td><td>

Now I say, "It is time for us to talk about how you all and I scored your final drafts. Mark the chart below for your final draft. Then let's talk about two things:

1. What you needed to understand in order for us to move our assessments closer together.
2. Why we scored a trait of writing the same. What was each of us considering in arriving at the same score?"

</td></tr>
</table>

Note: Our talk can help me see that you understand the standards of writing that I am teaching. When we differ in our assessment of a trait, you or I may see that we need to change our score. Together we will help reach the score that is the most accurate.

The trait	Your assessment compared to mine		
Personal voice	Lower	Same	Higher
Picture of people	Lower	Same	Higher
Picture of places	Lower	Same	Higher
Beginning	Lower	Same	Higher
Ending	Lower	Same	Higher
Proofreading	Lower	Same	Higher
Total score	Lower	Same	Higher

<table>
<tr><td>

LEARN

Record the elements and benefits that your class creates of strong use of a Final Evaluation Rubric.

</td><td>

So what do students learn from reviewing the self-assessment and your assessment on the same rubric? Listen in on Ms. Brewer's classroom of fifth-graders who are preparing for the Grade 5 Writing Assessment required by their state department of education.

</td></tr>
</table>

"Final Evaluation Rubrics help us talk about writing."
"Rubrics teach us the standards."
"Little words paint pictures, too."
"Pictures are the most important trait about writing."
"'Exceed' only takes a little more work than 'meets.'"
"Errors don't count so much."
"Rubrics score all the traits at once."

The benefits of the student-friendly rubrics listed by teachers at a coaching workshop:

- Saves time
- Simplifies the procedure
- Specific process for teachers
- Structured
- Teachable
- Reliable
- As unbiased as grading writing can be

Conclusion: Final evaluation rubrics can effectively appear throughout the writing process. When students see one before they start to pre-write, they get a clear mental picture of their end goal. When they apply one to their first draft, it leads them to consider all of the traits important in a final draft. When they apply one to their final draft, they receive clear instruction on what they should focus on for the next writing assignment.

Beyond the Working Portfolio

So the engine of student performance is started by students and approved (or adjusted) by teachers. Students clearly see themselves in charge of their fate. In a Writing Cycle, 100 marks the point at which students exceed a stated standard, expressed as teacher expectations. To students, 85 represents meeting the standard. Teachers respond to a student's self-assessment with intention and care, inspiring a conversation of formative assessment in points. Take a hypothetical example. Assume that Antoine is a student of yours. Figure 13.7 shows how the dialogue between him and you rolls out through each of the first six weekly writing tasks in the Working Portfolio of the Writing Cycle.

Over six weeks of writing tasks, you coach Antoine and each of your other students with ease, especially those whose writing shows either lack of engagement or understanding.

A sense of joy fills teachers as they conduct their orchestra of student writers. They direct them in rehearsals of the writing process, following the musical score of the Writing Cycle through one genre and then the next. At the conclusion of six weeks of rehearsals in formative assessment, it's time for the concert. The conductor-teachers tap their batons on their music stands and raise them high to the level of the standard of the writing genre so well rehearsed. Their students raise their writing instruments to their practiced positions. They are ready for the performance, a concert presentation where they all write together on command to the rhythm of the Unassisted Writing Sample. That is the subject of the next chapter.

Figure 13.7   Sample Dialogue with a Student

Week	Writing Tasks of a Writing Cycle	Total Possible	Antoine's Self-check	Your Response
1	1st Draft #1	100	85	82
2	1st Draft #2	100	100	95
3	1st Draft #3	100	85	88
4	Revision of one first draft	100	85	88
5	Proofreading of the final draft	100	100	90
6	Final evaluation of the final draft	100	94	90
	Average	100	92	89

1st Draft #1	Antoine logs ...	a ◎ (85): "I met your expectations."
	You insert ...	an 82: "Indeed you did—almost."
1st Draft #2	Antoine logs ...	+ (100): "I exceeded your expectations."
	You insert ...	a 95: "Yes, clearly so."
1st Draft #3	Antoine logs ...	a ◎ (85): "I met your expectations."
	You insert ...	an 88: "You met standard and a little more."
Revision	Antoine logs ...	a ◎ (85): "I met your expectations."
	You insert ...	an 88: "You met standard and a little more."
Proofreading	Antoine logs ...	+ (100), "I exceeded your expectations."
	You insert ...	a 90: "You did—by a small amount."
Final evaluation	Antoine logs ...	a 94: "I exceeded your expectations."
	You insert ...	a 90: "Yes you did—but by a small amount."

Looking Back

In your response journal, describe two ideas from the First Draft Response Form or Final Evaluation Rubric that were valuable for you in courses that you presently teach.

Looking Ahead

What things coming up in your curriculum invite you to use the First Draft Response Form or Final Evaluation Rubric?

Chapter 14

Write an Unassisted Writing Sample with Me

> **Common Core State Standards for Writing**
>
> Range of Writing—10. Write routinely over ... shorter time frames (a single sitting or a day or two) for a range of tasks, purposes and audiences.

"People never improve unless they look to some standard or example higher or better than themselves."

—Tryon Edwards

Up until now, you coached students in their knowledge of key practices of writing and invited them to write along with you from analyzing or creating a topic to scoring final drafts. All of those writing tasks focused on teaching students to write, helping students learn key practices of effective writing. Based on what we know about how language skills are learned, you focused on *know-how* knowledge first in each lesson and concluded it with a focus on *know-about* knowledge.

Know-how knowledge

Your students

- Studied your written model of the writing task
- Met or exceeded your quantified expectations for each writing task
- Read their writing aloud to a PAL

Know-about knowledge

Your students

- Self-assessed their performance based on your expectations.
- Listened to a PAL's writing and responded with a concrete routine that you provided (such as "The voice/pictures/flow [pick one] stood out in your writing. Here are the two parts of your writing to mark voice/pictures/flow [pick one].")

- Helped create the list of elements and benefits of a writing task at the close of each week

All of these tasks included support from teachers and peers; the assessment was formative. Now, the time has come for your students to break from real-time support and formative assessment and move to summative assessment of their Unassisted Writing Sample.

The Unassisted Writing Sample assesses what your students have learned in their experience with a writing genre. The eight-page booklet (see www.writingtowin.com) contains a minimum of the familiar elements of the Writing Cycle in the format and style of a test of written expression published by a state or national agency. Still, the best thing you can do as you administer this mock writing test is to write with your students. When students see you writing along with them, they follow you with engagement. They write what they are thinking. If you move about the room, they are tempted to ask, "Is this right?" just to hear you reply, "Sorry, I can't answer any questions."

The Unassisted Writing Sample does not include an assignment page or a word bank, but it does provide space to study the prompt, brainstorm possible responses and jot list before they begin to draft their thoughts. It also excludes a First Draft Response Form and peer-revision rubric, but it permits students to revise their first drafts in a different color of ink. The sample is best administered in two sections: section I for prewriting (15 minutes) and first draft (30 minutes), section II for revision (20 minutes), final draft (20 minutes) and proofreading (20 minutes). Students need a healthy bathroom break between sections scheduled on the same day. Otherwise, consider scheduling them on two consecutive days at the same time of day.

The design and schedule of the Unassisted Writing Sample prepares students for state testing in any state. Yet the Unassisted Writing Sample is more than preparation for a state testing experience. It assesses the complete standard of a genre of writing. In states like South Carolina and Florida that require students to write only first drafts, the two sections prepare them for practices that allows them to bring closure to their ideas. It also provides solid preparation for states like Oregon that require students to take their test on a computer in three 50-minute blocks on three consecutive days. The longer periods of time allow most students to elect the option of writing on a computer to use state-approved advanced organizers and word-level spell-check.

However you schedule this sample, the writing must be completely unassisted. Students move from the writing topic prompt to drafting in day one, then on to revision and creating a final draft and proofreading in day two with only an announcement from you at regular time windows to help them pace their progress.

The Final Evaluation Rubric for an Unassisted Writing Sample needs to be based directly on the rubric of your state. In Unassisted Writing Samples of all our client districts, we create a one-page version of a state rubric. States like Oregon present state rubrics of one page for each of six traits at six performance levels. Georgia presents a separate four-page rubric for each of three writing genres. We condensed the South Dakota state rubric from six pages (one for each trait) to one page, front and back. In this way, we were able to help teachers score final drafts with greater inter-rater reliability. Figure 14.1 (below) shows the Analytic Scoring Sheet.

Figure 14.1 Analytic Scoring Sheet

I. **Ideas and development:** The quantity and quality of ideas presented and how well they are elaborated and developed.

Extensive development of several ideas (or one important main idea) with extension and elaboration on all or most of the points. Uniqueness, interest to audience and strong supporting details. Exceptional or extremely thorough writing.	4	
Good development of ideas with many extended details. Ideas are fairly well supported.	3	
Adequately supported ideas with some details extended or elaborated.	2	
Weak ideas minimally supported with little or no extension of details.	I	

II. **Organization, unity and coherence:** Papers should demonstrate a smooth and logical progression. Digressions, if any, should be minimal. Transitions may contribute to the fluency of the paper.

Completely organized, with smooth flow from one idea to the next through transitions and sequencing. Unity is strongly evident, with no wandering from the primary theme or plan.	4	
Fairly well organized with unity. Some transitions. Little digression from main ideas or writing.	3	
Small amount of organization. Weak plan. Ideas only minimally connected. May frequently wander from expected writing mode.	2	
Little or no organization; a collection of random thoughts with little connection. Off topic; strays frequently from topic or mode.	I	

III. **Word choice:** The appropriateness, precision and "flavor" of the words chosen.

Precise, specific word choices, with correct meaning and appeal; may be vivid and imaginative.	4	

Word choices are appropriate and specific. May lack "sparkle," but the meaning is clear.	3	
Fair use of words, specific with little variety; may be simplistic or vague, but mostly effective.	2	
Very simplistic. Meaning may be unclear or inappropriate.	1	

IV. Sentences and paragraphs

Excellent control and formation of sentences. Variety of sentence structure, type and length contribute to fluency and interest. Paragraphs used where appropriate. Few errors.	4	
Adequate control of sentence formation. Some mix of sentence types, lengths and structures. Small number of errors that do not interfere with fluency. Some attempt at paragraphing.	3	
Most sentences constructed correctly. Little variety in type, length or structure and either monotonous or choppy. Several errors or lack of control. May have no attempt at paragraphing.	2	
Poor sentence structure with many errors that inhibit fluency or clarity. Lack of control.	1	

V. Grammar and usage: Includes subject-verb agreement, correct tense usage, pronoun agreement and usage.

Error-free or very few errors in proportion to the length of the paper.	4	
Good grammar and word usage. Errors do not detract from the overall quality of the paper.	3	
Fair grammar and usage. Errors may interfere with meaning. May be simplistic.	2	
Poor grammar and word usage, with frequent or serious errors.	1	

VI. Writing mechanics: Punctuation, capitalization and spelling.

Error free or very few errors in proportion to the length of the paper.	4	
Most punctuation, capitalization and spelling is correct. Errors do not affect meaning.	3	
Some errors in punctuation, capitalization and/or spelling; they may interfere with meaning.	2	
Frequent and/or serious errors in mechanics that interfere with communication.	1	

Some states report students' scores by trait without providing them an overall score. Such scores guide teachers in planning mini-lessons that focus on developing those traits. In our experience, students benefit more

Figure 14.2 South Dakota Grade 5 Results

	Ideas	Organization	Word	Sentences	Grammar	Mechanics
2003–2004	64	38	55	41	47	42
2004–2005	51	28	52	38	43	39
2005–2006	59	55	59	40	49	40
2006–2007	64	62	61	51	52	44

from an overall score that announces whether a student meets the standard performance level of a grade level. South Dakota's results for Grade 5 are shown in Figure 14.2.

Interestingly, these scores suggest that South Dakota teachers of fifth-graders began spending significant amounts of class time on matters of organization, sentences and grammar (usage) between 2003 and 2007. This data coincide with observations of our client elementary schools in the state.

The rubric in the Unassisted Writing Sample presented here is a one-page version of the Georgia state rubric for grades 3 through 12, *The Analytic Scoring System*, page 161 (see *A Writing Cycle for Writer's Workshop*, 4th ed., 2011, p. E-34). The rubric describes the state standard for each of four traits in the comments under the number 3. A score of 5 exceeds the standard, and a score of 2 approaches, but definitely misses, the standard. Tests of the condensed rubric on page 161 parallel the scores of sample student writing scored by the Georgia testing and reporting service.

Lesson with Scripting for an Unassisted Writing Sample

> **INVITE**
>
> *Write an Unassisted Writing Sample with me.*

Teacher: **Write an Unassisted Writing Sample with me.** Your peers, your teacher and I have supported you throughout the steps of the writing process for a genre of writing. We coached each other in analyzing our writing topic prompts and scoring our final draft with a Final Evaluation rubric. You scored a peer's final draft and a peer scored yours. Your teacher followed through by scoring all of your final drafts a second time. We learned from the experience the standard expectations for a genre of writing—narrative, persuasive or informational/expository writing. Now it's time for you to work through the writing process on your own. It is that simple, and you can do it. So let's get started.

<table>
<tr><td>

MODEL

Review the steps of the writing process with me.

</td><td>

Since this is a test of what you have learned from instruction in a writing genre, I won't read you a model final draft. From a distance, I'll hold up a model that I took through the writing process from prewriting to final draft. As I turn the pages, the names of each step of the writing process will appear on the interactive board to help you pace your writing today . . .

</td></tr>
</table>

- Prewriting (brainstorm and jot list)   20 minutes
- First draft   30 minutes

. . . and tomorrow . . .

- Revision   20 minutes
- Final draft   20 minutes
- Proofreading   10 minutes

As always, I invite you to write along with me. I am willing to write anything that I ask you to write. I have set the timer to sound a tone at the posted time limits, reminding you of the suggested pace that will help you reach standard expectations of a genre. The same suggested times appear in the Unassisted Writing Sample. I cannot answer any questions during this timed writing sample. It is time for you to show that you know what to do without help. You are well prepared and up to the task. Good luck.

<table>
<tr><td>

DO

Complete a first and final draft in your Unassisted Writing Sample booklet.

</td><td>

Day One: Unassisted Writing Sample

Teacher: Read through the writing topic prompt and prewrite your response to the topic on the space provided below the prompt. You have 20 minutes.

Teacher [20 minutes later]: If you have not completed your prewriting plan yet, it is time to move soon to writing your first draft on pages 3 to 4. You have 30 minutes to write out your thoughts on the two pages provided.

</td></tr>
</table>

Teacher [30 minutes later]: If you have not completed your first draft, it is time for you to finish it as best you can and hand in your Unassisted Writing Sample booklets. We shift to the regular schedule for the remainder of the day. Go home, eat well, sleep for a full eight hours and have a good breakfast in the morning in preparation for day two. This is the important day, since the faculty will read and score only final drafts. Yes, faculty members from math to PE are scoring student writing together each nine weeks.

Day Two: Unassisted Writing Sample

Teacher: I'm returning your first drafts. They are as finished as they will be for this sample. With a red pen in hand, reread your draft now with an eye for revision. You have 20 minutes to revise your first draft and make important improvements.

Teacher [20 minutes later]: It is time for you to start creating your final draft if you haven't already started. Use pages 5 to 6 of your Unassisted Writing Sample to write a final draft that includes your first draft with all revisions. You have 20 minutes. After 20 minutes, you have 10 minutes to proofread this final draft carefully.

Teacher [20 minutes later]: Take 10 additional minutes to finish proofreading. Then hand your final draft in for scoring by two teachers. The score of your final draft will count the weight of two writing assignments on your report card for ELA in this nine-week grading period.

Assessing the Final Draft of the Unassisted Writing Sample

> **LOOK**
> *Revise the way your final draft will be scored.*

In moving from a conventional assessment to standards-based assessment, the two forms of assessment remain side by side. Educators are moving intentionally toward standards-based assessment, while students and parents remain solidly in the world of the conventional A–F or 70 to 100 grading scale. Figure 14.5 shows a rubric with elements of both scales that highlights the prevailing

Figure 14.3   Analytic Scoring System Traits

Analytic Scoring System Traits	Writer's Workshop for the Common Core	Weight
Ideas	Pictures	40%
Organization	Flow	20%
Style	Voice	20%
Conventions	Surface errors	20%

Figure 14.4 Condensed Georgia Rubric

Analytic Scoring System: Georgia

Writer:

Evaluator:

Circle one comment and nearby number in each row that best describes how you judge each trait of writing in a final draft. Multiply the circled number by the points on the far right; place the product in the margin at the right. In the total raw score box, place the sum of the four numbers. Convert the raw score to the 70- to 100-point grading scale using the chart from the "Evaluating" section of your *Writing Cycle for Writer's Workshop* resource guide (see page 142 of this book). Change the comments to represent your assessment accurately.

Ideas (pictures)

1	2	3	4	5	x 8 pts =
Your writing may be off topic. Your main idea and supporting ideas are unclear or undeveloped. You did not write in the _____ genre.		Responds to the topic. You present a clear main idea. Your supporting ideas need clearer examples and details. You don't show that you are writing to an audience.		Unique response to the topic in the right genre; well-developed main idea. Your examples and details help me picture your thoughts. You write clearly to a specific audience.	

Organization (flow)

1	2	3	4	5	x 4 pts =
Ideas are not in a meaningful order. Ideas lack flow. Transitions are awkward. You seem to follow a formula for writing.		Pattern of organization is clear. Sequence of ideas makes sense but is not complete. Transitions are a little too obvious.		Your sequence of ideas is related to the main idea. Organization fits the _____ genre. Transitions are varied and smooth inside and between paragraphs.	

Style (voice)

1	2	3	4	5	x 4 pts =
You use vague or general words. Sentences are too much alike or confusing. Unclear point of view, personal voice or tone (like humorous, angry, excited or intelligent).		Satisfactory choice of words. I see some sentence variety. I sense a point of view, a personal voice and tone (like humorous, angry, excited, kind, clever, pleasant or intelligent).		Excellent choice of words. Point of view is clear. A clear personal voice. Effective variety of sentences. A clearly _____ tone.	

Conventions (surface errors)

1	2	3	4	5	x 4 pts =
Many incorrect sentence patterns. Many mistakes in spelling, punctuation and capitals. Errors make your writing hard to read.		Many correct sentence patterns of all sentence types. You made a good number of mistakes in spelling, punctuation and capitals. Yet your writing is easy to read.		Consistently correct sentence patterns in a variety of sentence types. Errors in spelling, punctuation, capitals and sentence patterns are hard to find.	

Score converted to a 70- to 100-point scale: _____   **Total raw score:** _____

Figure 14.5 Correlations to the Analytic Scoring System

Raw Score	Score converted to 70- to 100-point scale	Standard	Score on Analytic Scoring System
Below 40	Below 70	Misses standard	1–2
40–59	70–79	Approaching standard	2–3
60–79	80–89	Meets standard	3–4
80–100	90–100	Exceeds standard	5

scale of a given school district or school. For students, I simply announce, "Your final draft is scored by two teachers using your state writing rubric. In the state of Georgia, the state writing rubric, *The Analytic Scoring System*, includes these four traits of writing."

The average raw score of two teachers converts to a converted score based on the conversion chart on page 142.

A Further Option

A number of teachers have found benefit in letting PALs score the final drafts of their Unassisted Writing Samples. Consider this after students have experienced teacher evaluations of at least two or three Unassisted Writing Samples. Teachers report that PALs' evaluations helped their students speak the language of the state standards sooner. It is wonderful to see some PALs coach each other, showing full understanding of how the scoring rubric represents the stated standard for a genre of writing. I understand and trust the move to PALs' scoring of the summative assessment. For the students' sake, this move needs to be made at just the right time.

Note: The rubric on page 161 is generic. You may want to insert a different comment for the trait of ideas (picture) in different genres. For example, the comment under "3" for meeting the standard changes for

- Narrative genre: clear plot and some development of character
- Informational/expository genre: controlling idea that explains or describes the assigned topic
- Persuasive genre: clear, fully described position on the assigned topic
- Comment under "5," exceeds the standard
- Narrative genre: well-developed plot and characters

Figure 14.6 Conversion Chart
(converting raw scores to a 70- to 100-point scale)

If the raw score is:	The converted score is:			If the raw score is:	The converted score is:
100	100		Meets	64	82
98	99	E		62	81
96	98	X		60	80
94	97	C	A	58	79
92	96	E	P	56	78
90	95	E	P	54	77
88	94	D	R	52	76
86	93	S	O	50	75
84	92		A	48	74
82	91		C	46	73
80	90		H	44	72
78	89		E	42	71
76	88	M	S	40	70
74	87	E		38	69
72	86	E	Does	36	68
70	85	T	Not	34	67
68	84	S	Meet	32	66
66	83			30	65

- Informational/expository genre: clear controlling idea that fully describes or explains the assigned topic
- Persuasive genre: well-developed controlling idea that establishes the validity of the writer's position

Be willing to adjust the language of any standard rubric to help students communicate in the language of the standard.

So what will your students learn from reviewing the assessment of their teachers on a timed test of written expression? Listen in on a classroom of eighth-graders who felt the approach of their state's Grade 8 Writing Assessment.

"The teachers' score tells us if we met the standard."
"Rubrics make it easy to understand my score."
"Writing samples are genre tests."
"Each trait in writing is important."
"This is a real test of writing."
"'Pictures' are the most important trait."
"'Exceed' is just a little better than 'meets.'"
"Why don't errors count so much?"

Benefits of the rubric listed by teachers include:

- Frequent use teaches the language of the standard to students.
- Scoring, not grading saves time.
- It's a simplified procedure for non-ELA teachers to follow.
- It's a well-specified process for teachers.
- Structure focuses on one trait at a time.
- Teachable because of the graphic simplicity.
- Reliable; it promotes consensus.
- It is as unbiased as grading can be.

Conclusion: Once you have completed a list of the elements and benefits of the Unassisted Writing Sample, help your students conclude that the Unassisted Writing Sample is a test of what we really know about a genre of writing. It sums up our performance in written expression and tells us what we still need to work on.

Using Final Evaluation Rubrics from State or National Standards

Scoring student writing with rubrics can be a huge time-saver. When appropriate procedures are followed, a 250- to 300-word final draft can be scored by two separate teachers in half the time it takes one teacher to score it using the "mark and comment-in-the-margins" routine. In several schools that I serve, the full faculty commits to scoring their students' writing two to four times a year. Teachers arrange themselves five to a table as shown in Figure 14.7. A stack of unscored student papers is placed in one stack at end of the table. A rubric printed on both sides of a page is placed next to the student drafts. Once raters have scored a paper using the rubric on one side, they turn the rubric over and place it in a stack to be scored by another rater at the table. Once the draft has been scored twice, it moves to the table leader. Table leaders tally up the score of both raters and read the paper a third time if the two raters disagree by more than 15 out of 100 points. The last faculty I assisted in scoring Unassisted Writing Samples completed scoring all students' writing in under 2 hours, and the students received an objective assessment of their writing 72 hours after they had written their papers. The students were happy; the teachers, especially the ELA teachers who usually have the job of scoring papers alone, were ecstatic. In fact, here are the conclusions that they drew from the Reliable Scoring Session.

- It helped me be more objective overall, and it did not let the mechanics and grammar distort my judgment.
- It helped me understand the state standards.
- It was less time-consuming than regular grading.
- It gives students feedback quickly in the language of the standard.
- It shows what help students need and guides re-teaching.
- It confirms my assessment with the assessment of others.
- It lets us know if we need to tighten up or lighten up on our expectations of students.
- Students have the benefit of agreement of teachers.
- Teachers know that expectations are more consistent throughout the school.
- It helps us see glaring shortcomings in teaching and/or learning.
- The quicker we scored, the more consistent we became.
- I got over my fear that others would find out I was insecure about the way I assessed writing.

It seems that whether students self-assess the final drafts of their Unassisted Writing Samples or not, the experience of summative assessment induces them to talk with us significantly about the Common Core State

Figure 14.7 Rating System

Standards for writing in the language of the standards. There is no doubt that such conversation is a certain benefit for students and teachers alike.

Looking Back

In your response journal, describe two ideas from a Final Evaluation Rubric and Reliable Scoring Session in this chapter that were valuable for you as a teacher in courses that you presently teach.

Looking Ahead

What things coming up in your curriculum invite you to use a Final Evaluation Rubric or Reliable Scoring Session?

Chapter 15

Publish a Final Draft with Me

Common Core State Standards for Writing

Range of Writing—10. Write routinely over extended time frames (time for research, reflection and revision) for a range of discipline-specific tasks, purposes and audiences.

Production and Distribution of Writing—5. Develop and strengthen writing as needed by planning, revising, editing, rewriting or trying a new approach.

Production and Distribution of Writing—6. Use technology, including the Internet, to produce and publish writing and to interact and collaborate with others.

"Recognition: babies cry of it, grown men die for it."

—Anonymous

Your students have written two final drafts in a target writing genre. The quarter has come to an end. The nine-week grade report that goes to parents presents classroom assessments that are

- Formative—evidence that students worked through the expectations of six writing tasks of the standard of the genre
- Summative—evidence that their unassisted performance in a writing genre approached, met or exceeded the standards of that genre

The nine-week report represents an important motivating tool for many students, but it pales by comparison with simple recognition. Recognizing students' writing by publishing it may be the single most powerful task of the writing process—and unfortunately, it is the one that is most often left out of classroom routines. Certainly, posting student exemplars throughout the writing process is a form of publishing. But this chapter looks at easy routines for presenting students' final drafts to an audience that "talks" back to them in specific, productive ways. When your students publish their writing to a responsive audience instead of an imagined one, you will marvel at the empowering energy of publishing that touches each of them. Students look forward to publishing after the first authentic experience with it. They look around at the different publishing places and strategies that show up in their school and ask to start making their own choices for publishing their writing themselves. Your role? To introduce new ideas about where and how they publish. Devote a week each quarter to publishing and see what happens. Some of your students will come up with better ideas than the one you present. That can only be a good thing.

Publishing writing always includes:

1. An audience other than the classroom teacher. Examples include a real or imaginary pen pal, a relative to whom the writing is actually sent, a teacher of students at the same or higher grade level, students from another class and adults from the community.
2. Sudents from different schools.
3. Students' illustrations and an opportunity for integrating writing and art. The integration, however, must complement the purpose of the writing. Illustrations may be as simple as bright construction paper on which final drafts are mounted for display, digital photos from a family or school camera, clever clip art discovered online or computer-generated images that some students create out of class.

I have witnessed an enormous variety of successful publishing strategies in the schools I serve. Some of them are described in this chapter. Don't be overwhelmed by the sheer number of them; they are options for your choosing. I have either witnessed them in use successfully or gotten them to work for me, adding my own nuances where necessary. So start small, with one idea or two dictated by the physical limits of your building or school policies. Repeat them until they are refined for easy use and start adding ever-widening possibilities for publishing to your archive.

The Standard for Publishing Writing

When students know that someone other than you will read their final drafts, they work harder to do their best. Displaying final drafts outside of your classroom, and even outside of the school, energizes students to package their writing in creative ways. During a school year, display their final drafts in hallways used by students from other grade levels for at least two quarters. This can include displays of elementary student writing in a nearby middle school and displays of middle school student writing in elementary schools. Displays in professional offices, retail stores or other school buildings provide remarkable motivation but take more time and advance planning. Simple strategies provide finishing touches to the writing. The spotlight for any presentation of final drafts is the writing, not the trimmings of publication. All ideas for publication must complement or complete the writing, not compete or distract from it.

Publication Strategies

The most effective publication strategies assign student audiences concrete, easy-to-complete response tasks. The responses must be written in the concise terms of writing used in your classroom mini-lessons and close activities. The following publication strategies, which satisfy these requirements, are not by any means comprehensive; they are intended to seed publishing strategies you come up with that stay with the limits of your school facility and policies. Just remember to try each strategy you choose more than once before you move on to the next one. When you come up with specific, productive strategies yourself, let us know at author@eyeoneducation.com.

1. In a prominent in-school display outside your classroom, post the final drafts of all the students who met your expectations for publication. Invite two colleagues to bring a class of their students to visit the display and respond to the writing in a specifically designed routine. Each visiting student arrives with a card on which you place the student numbers of three students (use no names) (Figure 15.1). Without conferring with one another, all students in the visiting class

Figure 15.1   Student Card

Student Number	"The voice, pictures or flow reached me as I read your draft." [List one below.]	Quote evidence to support your choice from the paper.
1578		
1579		
1580		

Signed _____

fill out their cards and return them to their teacher for review before they are handed to you.

2. Identify excellence in voice, pictures, flow and/or surface features. A simple button, ribbon or badge that you create with clip art on your computer can announce

Excellence in Writing Voice
Excellence in Written Pictures
Excellence in Writing Flow
Excellence in Surface Features of Writing

Award recognition to all of the published drafts that actually show evidence of exceeding your expectation for these four traits of writing. Some papers may receive more than one award. I'd be delighted to hear that you had to award two to four awards to every student in your classes.

3. Ask people from the community known to some of the students to adopt one of your classes for the duration of a Writing Cycle. Make sure they are willing to write along with the class, especially on the first and last days of the cycle. On the first day, the visitors are introduced and interviewed in relation to the writing topic prompt. On the last day, they listen to the student writing, respond using a PALS strategy and share some writing of their own.

4. Let your fourth-grade students take a field trip to a first-grade class. Partnered with their first-grade PAL, they help shape a final draft into a published piece that is proofread, presented or illustrated. Your students take more care in their own writing by guiding the writing habits of younger students.

5. Arrange for your eighth-graders to visit their future high school early in the school year. Partnered with a eleventh- or twelfth-grade PAL in a college prep course, they will help shape their high school counterpart as much as the high schoolers help them. The benefits of visits to upper grades comes from second-graders visiting fifth-graders and fifth-graders visiting eighth-graders. Note the minimum spread between grades is three years.

6. Integrate three drafts of a Working Portfolio into an annual science, social studies or health project required of students to place on public display in your school.

Publication Places

Publication places need not be exotic. Choose places where students can see their writing meet a live audience. I am continually amazed at the significant impact written responses from an audience have on students' writing; it can last for months and even years.

The classroom

Invite visitors into the class to write with or respond to students as part of a Writing Cycle.

1. **Writer's Block:** Devote an entire wall, from floor to ceiling, to display student exemplars throughout the writing process. Make certain the space is large enough to accommodate all of the students you teach. There is nothing more important than displaying student writing for others to read and enjoy. Consider sections in the display for approaching, meeting and exceeding the standard of the genre. Watch your students point with pride as their writing progress from section to section. During the year, watch the "Exceeds the Standard" section grow and the "Approaches the Standard" section shrink to the point that you remove the label from the wall. The Writer's Block has worked its magic.

2. **Classroom binders for publication:** All students whose drafts meet standard qualify to publish their final drafts in a binder displayed prominently on a counter or shelf in the classroom. As the next final draft is published in a class binder, the current one moves to an archive of previous classroom binders for publication on an easy-to-access shelf. Writing in a binder may focus on
   a. A single writing topic prompt that correlates to the standards of a state or national test of written expression
   b. The writing genre of a current Writing Cycle
   c. Exemplars of students' final drafts collected in Writing Cycles and Unassisted Writing Samples throughout the current school year

3. **Classroom Web site, blog or wiki.** These formats make it easy for students to read one another's work. In addition, family members and friends in other classes can read a student's work. Students will edit their work more carefully when they know it might be seen by the outside world.

The school

Invite visitors into the school building to write with or respond to students as part of a Writing Cycle. Employees of youth programs, county extension offices, the Department of Family and Children Services and similar agencies are often glad to assist by visiting and responding to students' writing. They need to know the purpose of their visit and receive written directions for their task before arriving. Such visits provide students with natural reasons for writing notes of appreciation or thank-you notes.

4. **The Great Write-On Wall:** One entire side of a cafeteria or multi-purpose room can become a place to display each classroom's top-notch writing. Teachers designate three to five spots in which they display the writings of the students who deserve or earn recognition for the current Writing Cycle. The wall can change in theme every nine weeks. Student artwork can be intermingled at the direction of the school's art teacher.

5. **Annual writing festival:** Each class (or homeroom) is responsible for setting up a booth that will attract students to write on a specific topic, mode or theme. Students rotate through the festival for no more than 60 to 90 minutes at a time. Be careful. Festival atmospheres can fuel cutesy, trivial writing tasks. Make sure that the writing at each booth requires the rigor of prewriting, drafting, revising, proofreading, evaluating or publishing as presented in the key practices in previous chapters. The student body meets the last hour of the day or the first hour of the next day to hear the best writing from each of the booths. Writing festivals provide cost-efficient field trips in tight economic times.

6. **Teachers write, too!** This is the most energizing of all the publishing ideas I have witnessed. A bulletin board display in a well-trafficked hallway or cafeteria is filled with teachers' writing; it may also include the writing of other adults at the school.

7. **School publications:** During a selected week, students from one class or grade display self-made books on library tables. Following the week of display, the media specialist and teachers select several of the books to accession and place on the library shelves for regular checkout.

8. **Parents write, too:** If you are interested in boosting parent involvement in your parent-school organization, consider this strategy. When the writing tasks are concrete, specific and easy to follow, more parents than you would expect enjoy writing for and with their own children. Parent-student teams may work on in-class or at-home writing tasks. Recognize these efforts at a parent-teacher-student meeting. Be prepared. Once parent involvement grows large enough, you will need to devise a method for selecting a limited number of writings to present to the parents, teachers and students gathered. When students are on the program at a parent night, parents will show up.

Outside of school

Once students are comfortable publishing their writing for audiences within their school, help them share their writing with the community at large. I've witnessed these publishing ideas work extremely well.

9. Place your students' writing in the buildings of school sponsors, business establishments (such as banks or supermarkets) and government institutions (the courthouse or parks and recreation pavilions). Let writing be its own announcement to the community. Once the writing is up, the word of its publication spreads.
10. Report, short story and poetry opportunities abound among nationally published magazines, but the percent of submitted entries published is small. Since the qualifications for submissions are usually rigorous, recognize all of your students whose writing meets the qualification for submission. The occasional published entry is just icing on the cake of publication.
11. Local writing contests abound. Many of them promote black history, state or local heritage, great Americans, the values of garden clubs, various civic groups, the Daughters of the American Revolution and the like. Unlike the rigorous requirements for national publications, the requirements for these contests may be less well-defined. In that case, specify expectations yourself before you invite students to participate.

In all of the above strategies, locations and opportunities, be sure to maintain the use of the instructional tools presented in previous chapters. Let students select the tools they use from archives of writing tools such as *A Writing Cycle for Writer's Workshop* (2011). Once you have guided students through two or three Writing Cycles, your students will impress you with their confident choices about their own writing.

Publication need no longer be ignored or deleted from classroom routines. It needn't present a great burden of effort and time. It is simply the last step of a Writing Cycle that carries value for your students, and therefore, for you. Recognition has a far longer lasting impact on students than any other single step of the writing process. That's precisely why we include hints of recognition throughout the cycle. Publication to

- A PAL (read their writing aloud verbatim) at the close of daily work sessions
- Small groups at the end of a weekly writing task
- Their teachers for a response on the First Draft Response Form
- A peer at the close of a revision task
- A peer-for-peer evaluation of final drafts

- The whole class during the quarter for celebration and a cheer
- An audience outside of the classroom and/or school

When you post student work throughout the tasks of a Writing Cycle, you satisfy an essential feature of standards-based learning: posting student exemplars of work that approaches, meets and exceeds a standard. So involve other teachers, administrators, students and parents in simply designed publication plans.

Benefits

From the first time students receive a live and written response from an audience, they see and feel immeasurable benefits. Listen in on a classroom of third-graders at E. C. West Elementary School.

"It was scary the first time kids read my paper."
"The comments are always good."
"I can't wait to publish again. Is that how to say it?"
"Can we publish at the middle school like the fifth graders do?"
"Let's show our writing in the little kids' hall next time."
"I want to use my armadillo story; can I?"
"Can we publish again tomorrow?"
"When are you going to publish your story, Ms. Smith?"

Benefits of publishing listed by teachers include:

- I never would have guessed publishing could be so easy. The adults and kids did their parts.
- There was genuine excitement for the writers and the responders.
- Students show more excitement about the next time they write after a publishing event.
- It saves time in the long run and speeds up the next Writing Cycle.
- Parents were eager to share in the responsibility.
- Extended families showed up to see their students' writing recognized.
- Writing Cycle routines for publishing provide specific routines for teachers to follow.
- Publishing had been a kind of free-for-all before. Quantified routines make for orderly students.
- These strategies are easy to teach to students.

Conclusion: Help your students sum up their publishing experiences in one of these sentences.

- When we all do our part in the plan for publishing, it is both instructive and entertaining.

- When readers in our audience tell us what parts they enjoyed and what parts were strong, we feel like writing again.

Looking Back

In your response journal, describe two ideas about publication strategies and places that were valuable for you as a teacher in courses that you presently teach.

Looking Ahead

What things coming up in your curriculum invite you to use the remarkable power of recognition in publishing writing?

A Prediction for You

As I began to write this epilogue, I learned that the students at a school that has faithfully used our Writing Cycles packets for two years posted a 93% pass rate on a state writing assessment (the top quartile of schools in the state). The year before its students met the Writing Cycle (Working Portfolios and Unassisted Writing Samples), the pass rate was 46% (bottom quartile). At a second school, 23% of its students exceeded the target on a state writing assessment (three times the state average). An e-mail from a third school came from a special education teacher who team-teaches in three ELA classes with included students. She celebrated the fact that all of the special needs students met standard on the state writing test after two years of using the Writing Cycle. The difference between these three schools and those listed in chapter 5? None of these schools received on-site professional development from a certified trainer. Their use of the Writing Cycle began with one teacher attending a coaching workshop one time and returning to school to set up a model classroom. In the course of a year, others visited the model classroom and asked to replicate the model in their own classrooms, and the rigorous routines for writing began to expand throughout the school. Significant increases in student performance followed close behind.

Writer's Workshop for the Common Core presents the same basic professional development of the Writing to Win Coaching Workshops. When you download instructional tools from www.eyeoneducation.com or purchase copies of a *Writing Cycle for Writer's Workshop* for teachers and *Writing Cycle Packets* for students from www.writingtowin.com, the benefits for you and your students are just nine weeks away. I feel confident in the following prediction.

You Partner with a PAL and Set Up Model Classrooms

Yes, just like students who learned best from sharing what they have learned with peers in regular coaching routines, you partnered with a

PAL to accelerate your learning curves in using writer's workshop with ease. Your PAL and you read through *Writer's Workshop for the Common Core* together, accepting and providing peer-coaching through a nine-week Writing Cycle. Before you started, you both set in place instructional tools and strategies as described in chapters 1 through 5.

- The Writing Cycle wall charts (chapter 3) set a productive pace for your students as they moved through the writing process.
- Students followed your leads, working and recording their progress in their own Working Portfolios from www.writingtowin.com. The portfolios included these key instructional tools:

  ○ Writing Cycle for Student Self-Check (chapter 3)
  ○ Assignment page and word bank that students completed and self-assessed for each of three first drafts (chapters 6 and 7)
  ○ First Draft Response Form with your suggested revision and proofreading strategies (chapters 9–12)
  ○ Final Evaluation Rubrics that students scored before you did for the modes of writing that students chose to publish (chapters 6 and 13)

- The following posters, like those from www.writingtowin.com, kept you and your students focused on the key practices for learning to write.

  ○ Why we write to learn (Figure 1.2, p. 9)
  ○ Voice, pictures and flow (Figure 5.2, p. 38)
  ○ Picture makers (Figure 8.3, p. 66)
  ○ Picture killers (Figure 8.1, p. 64)
  ○ Descriptions of what prewriting, drafting, revising, proofreading, evaluating and publishing include (Chapter 6–14)

- From floor to crown molding, the full wall of your classrooms provided ample space to post the writing of all students as they moved through the Writing Cycle.

Your PAL and you followed the steps of the writing process through a first Writing Cycle as it was presented in chapters 6 through 8 and chapters 12 and 13. You both used the scripts without hesitation, sometimes reading them directly to your students. You told your classes, "Dr. Combs provided the scripts for us to use. The scripts work every time that he uses them as they are written. So we're following them just like he wrote them." You both did, and so did your classes. They believed in the power of the scripts. You saw that the power was actually the innate writing abilities of your student awakening within them. As you moved into the second

Writing Cycle, the scripts morphed into authentic invitations to write with you, replete with your own teaching style.

At the end of each Writing Cycle, your PAL and you reviewed

- Your observations of one another throughout the cycle.
- Student artifacts from the Writing Cycle.

Then you both completed the table of key practices in Figure E.1, to measure each other's fidelity in following the principles of *Writer's Workshop for the Common Core.*

Building Administrators in Your Model Classrooms

While you and your PAL worked through the Writing Cycle with your students, your administrators visited your classrooms and wrote along with you and your students. They stored their writing in Working Portfolios that you kept in your classrooms. They saw and experienced firsthand the power of writing as a way to learn. They returned more often than you expected, but especially at the end of the Writing Cycle, when they participated as authors in the final publication Author's Chair.

Parents visited your model classrooms because their students talked more about what they were learning in school than ever before. When they visited, their children showed them exemplars of completed Working Portfolios that 1) approached the state standard for writing, 2) met the state standard for writing or 3) exceeded the state standard for writing. They showed their parents how their final drafts in the Working Portfolio differed from the final draft of the Unassisted Writing Sample. They spoke of the voice, pictures and flow in their writing. Some of the students showed how much their writing had improved from before the Writing Cycle.

Your administrators watched all of these things with curiosity followed by satisfaction. They asked your PAL and you to help create a plan for extending the use of the Writing Cycle to other classrooms in your school, in due time. An idea as powerful as the Writing Cycle is worth implementing in a timely and productive fashion.

The Plan for Professional Learning Teams

The plan for expanding the design of your model writing classroom throughout your school came about with all deliberate care and intention. It resembled what you met in *Writer's Workshop for the Common Core*, but it varied in ways important for you and your students without sacrificing the faithful emphasis of the five key practices. Your PAL and you each

Figure E.1 Data Collector for Five Key Practices of the Writing Cycle (Q-MAPS)

Teacher _____ School _____

Month(s)/Year _____ Grade/subject _____

No.	Practice	Total number of writing tasks →	
1	**Q**uantified Teacher Expectations	listed on the Writing Cycle Log for Teacher Expectations (up to nine tasks).	_____
2	**M**odel Teacher Writing	written by teachers for/with their students.	_____
3	**A**uthentic Student Writing	required of students for each task.	_____
4	**P**ALS read aloud and respond	Students read the product of their writing task aloud to peers verbatim; peers identify voice, pictures or flow in the shared writing or use another PALS strategy.	_____
5	**S**tudent Self-Assessment	that empowers students to self-check their performance accurately using the +/◎/▭ method or similar rubric for each task.	_____

TASKS

Check all that are completed.

Teaching the Genre

Task 1 __Prewriting for 1st Draft #1
       __1st Draft #1
Task 2 __Prewriting for 1st Draft #2
       __1st Draft #2
Task 3 __Prewriting for 1st Draft #3
       __1st Draft #3

Teaching the Genre

Task 4 __Revision of one first draft
Task 5 __Proofreading one final draft
Task 6 __Evaluation of final draft with a rubric
Task 7 __Publishing a final draft
Task 8 __ Administer Unassisted Writing Sample
Task 9 __ Scoring Unassisted Writing Sample

Summary note: _____

led a professional learning team (PLT) of committed teachers who agreed to join your teams of four to seven members. You led them through the reading of *Writer's Workshop for the Common Core*, using the professional learning sessions at a pace determined by your group. You took it slowly this time—it actually took your PLT eleven weeks to complete a Writing Cycle. (Your PAL's PLT maintained the nine-week pace.) Although the two teams scheduled four one-hour meetings during the quarter, informal visits and exchanges among the members of the PLT occurred daily. Each member of your PLT felt that the design and implementation of a model classroom in their classes succeeded. Student performance data on independent tests of written expression verified that success.

Monitoring Tools as Communication

What was most satisfying for you, your PAL and your PLT members was how your view of administrative monitoring changed. In previous initiatives, administrative walk-throughs felt like the bosses checking up on the employees. Yet for some reason, the following monitoring tools felt and worked like critical vehicles of communication for teachers and administrators alike.

- Data Collector for Five Key Practices of the Writing Cycle. The same tool that you and your PAL used to coach each another continued to provide essential communication in charting progress and requesting help.
- Your administrators studied the sample Google.com form from Battlefield Elementary School (Figure E.2) and asked your media specialist to adjust it for use at your school. They allowed your two PLTs to communicate progress seamlessly and request help in fine-tuning their use of the Writing Cycle. It was satisfying for teachers to know that when they clicked "Submit" at the end of the form, the data automatically populated a spreadsheet at www.google.docs for your building administrators to access. Your administrators wisely gave your district administrators and regional educational consultants access to the spreadsheets for their edification and support.

Monitoring the progress of students and teachers in the Writing Cycle became a priority. It began as a quarterly report that students and teachers both anticipated. Later, your administrators inserted monthly, then weekly and daily recognition of exemplary writing during the morning announcements as the wave of exemplary writing grew. A schoolwide celebration marked the report of student performance on tests of written expressions like those reported in chapter 5. You took time to report the data of your experiences to your district office, your local newspaper and the folks at Eye On Education (author@eyeoneducation.com).

Figure E.2   Battlefield Elementary Writing Cycle
Data Collection

Teachers, please complete this form every nine weeks to report progress and request assistance.

* Required

Grading Period *Check the appropriate box.

❑ 1st nine weeks

❑ 2nd nine weeks

❑ 3rd nine weeks

❑ 4th nine weeks

Name* | Camp, David   ▼ |

Grade *Check all that apply.

❑ Third Grade

❑ Fourth Grade

❑ Fifth Grade

❑ Departmentalized

❑ Reading/Language Arts

❑ Math

❑ Science

❑ Social Studies

❑ Standard Homeroom

How many writing tasks did your students need to complete in your classroom this nine weeks?*
(Please enter quantity, e.g. 7, 9, etc.) |_____|

How many writing tasks did your students actually complete in your classroom during these nine
weeks?* (Please enter quantity, e.g. 7, 9, etc.) |_____|

How many of the writing tasks did you model in your own writing for your class?* (Please enter
quantity, e.g. 7, 9, etc.) |_____|

How many writing tasks did you list on the Writing Cycle wall chart with clearly defined
expectations for students?* (Please enter quantity, e.g. 7, 9, etc.) |_____|

How many writing tasks did your students self-assess with a plus, target or bar.* (Please enter
quantity, e.g. 7, 9, etc.) |_____|

How many writing tasks did your students share with a PAL or cooperative partner?* (Please
enter quantity, e.g. 7, 9, etc.) |_____|

Figure E.2   Battlefield Elementary Writing Cycle Data Collection

(continued)

How many writing tasks elicited authentic writing from your students?* Choose from

the list.

| 11% ▼ |
| 22% |
| 33% |
| 44% |
| 55% |
| 66% |
| 77% |
| 88% |
| 100% |

What writing genre did you use in implementing the Writing Cycle process-writing routine?* Check all that apply.

❑ A. Narrative

❑ B. Expository/informational

❑ C. Persuasive

❑ D. Response to literature (fiction)

❑ E. Response to literature (nonfiction)

❑ F. Research paper

❑ G. Imaginative writing (short story)

❑ H. Imaginative writing (poetry)

❑ I. Resume

❑ J. Business letter

❑ L. Personal letter

❑ M. Abstract of a source

❑ Other: _____

I need help in the following areas of extended-process writing. (Check all that apply.)

❑ Implementing certain writing tasks (prewriting, revision, proofreading, assessment)

❑ Students sharing and responding

❑ Timing and time for process writing

❑ Maintaining Writing Cycle wall chart and student portfolios and samples

❑ Modeling process-writing tasks for my students in my own writing

❑ Other: _____

A Scope and Sequence of Writing Tasks Across Grades and Subjects

Wisely, your administrators saw the need for creating a pacing guide and a scope and sequence of writing tasks for your school's expanding Writing Cycle network. Following the lead of the Common Core State Standards, they included all grades and subject areas. During their years at your school, the students met a variety of modes of writing in narrative, persuasive and expository genres. Your plan began with the example from E. C. West Elementary and Bear Creek Middle School (Atlanta, GA), where teachers in grades 1 through 8 committed to the scope and sequence shown in Figure E.3 on the next page.

Beyond the Walls of Your school

After completing two years of making the work of writer's workshop easier with your version of the Writing Cycle, you submitted a program proposal to a district, area, state or regional conference of a professional organization. Your presentation modeled the use of the instructional tools that you adopted and adapted as well as the resulting student performance data. In sharing your experiences in the teaching of writer's workshop with ease—the successes, the problems and their solutions—your implementation of the writer's workshop model increased in rigor and effectiveness. As interested teachers from the audiences in your presentations contacted you for help, their classes became new audiences for your writing and your students' writing. Your technology support person helped your teams describe your experiences and instructional tools on your school's Web site. The interest among teachers that you awakened by demonstrating how writer's workshop could be rolled out with ease kept your growing network of teachers of writing in a creative, productive mode as they continued to invite their students to write with them.

This is my vision for you. And this prediction has become a reality for numerous teachers who work the key practices with fidelity. Take the writing tasks offered in these pages one at a time. Stay with the first task until it shows evidence of all key practices. Work the key practices one at a time until they all feel natural. The journey of your teaching career began with a critical first step. The journey of easing the tasks in the teaching of writing is the same. I predict a beneficial and productive journey of employing writer's workshop for the Common Core State Standards.

Figure E.3 Scope and Sequence for Teaching Writing

Grade	Feature	First Quarter	Second Quarter	Third Quarter	Fourth Quarter
	Genre	Narrative	Informative/ Expanatory	Opinion	Response to Literature
1	Modes	Personal memory (3)	Character sketch (3)	Support an opinion (2), mirror poetry	Character sketch, description of setting, plot summary
	Revision	Jot and blend	Combining sentences, leads	Circling picture sentences	All three
	Proofreading	Pairs	Pairs	Pairs	Pairs
	Publishing	In-class	Hallway, pen pals	Nearby elementary school	Pen pals
	Subject area	ELA	ELA, social studies, science	ELA (2), social studies	ELA (2), science
2	Modes	Personal memory (2), imagining a story	Explain a process (3)	Support an opinion (2), business letter	Character sketch, description of setting, plot summary
	Revision	Jot and blend	Combining sentences, leads	Circling picture sentences	As needed
	Proofreading	Pairs	Triads	Triads	Triads
	Publishing	In-class	Hallway, pen pals	Business partner	Pen pals
	Subject area	ELA	ELA, math, science	ELA (2), social studies	ELA (2), science
3	Modes	Personal memory, imagining a story, historical narrative	Support an opinion (2), support a solution	Compare and contrast (3)	Nonfiction: summary, character sketch, explain a solution
	Revision	Jot and blend; leads	Circling picture sentences, leads	Combining sentences, writing leads, closes	As needed
	Proofreading	Triads	Triads	Sentence Check Chart	Sentence Check Chart

Figure E.3   Scope and Sequence for Teaching Writing
(continued)

Grade	Genre	Narrative	Opinion	Informative/ Explanatory	Response to Literature
3	Publishing	Hallway, pen pals	Business partner	Nearby middle school	Classroom binder
	Subject area	ELA (2), social studies	ELA, social studies	Math, science, social studies	ELA, social studies, science
4	Modes	Personal memory (3)	Character sketch (3)	Support an opinion (2), mirror poetry	Character sketch, description of setting, plot summary
	Revision	Jot and blend	Combining sentences, leads	Circling picture sentences	All three
	Proofreading	Pairs	Pairs	Pairs	Pairs
	Publishing	In-class	Hallway, pen pals	Nearby elementary school	Pen pals
	Subject area	ELA	ELA, social studies, science	ELA (2), social studies	ELA (2), science
5	Modes	Personal memory (2), imagining a story	Explain a process (3)	Support an opinion (2), business letter	Character sketch, description of setting, plot summary
	Revision	Jot and blend	Combining sentences, leads	Circling picture sentences	As needed
	Proofreading	Pairs	Triads	Triads	Triads
	Publishing	In-class	Hallway, pen pals	Business partner	Pen pals
	Subject area	ELA	ELA, math, science	ELA (2), social studies	ELA (2), science
6	Modes	Description, narration, imaginative writing	Support an opinion (3)	Character sketch (3)	Explain a process, contrast and compare (2)
	Revision	Jot and blend, writing leads	Circling picture sentences, writing leads	Combining sentences, writing leads, closes	As needed

Figure E.3 Scope and Sequence for Teaching Writing
(continued)

Grade	Genre	Narrative	Argument	Informative/ Explanatory	Response to Literature
6	Proofreading	Triads	Triads	Sentence Check Chart	Sentence Check Chart
	Publishing	Hallway, pen pals	Business partner	Nearby elementary school	Classroom binder
	Subject area	ELA (2), social studies	ELA, social studies	Math, science, social studies	ELA, social studies, science
7	Modes	Character sketch, narration, imaginative writing	Support an opinion (3)	Support a solution (2), compare and contrast	Compare and contrast (2), character sketch
	Revision	Jot and blend, leads	Circling picture sentences, leads	Combining sentences, writing leads, closes	As needed
	Proofreading	Triads	Triads	Sentence Check Chart	Sentence Check Chart
	Publishing	Hallway, pen pals	Business partner	Nearby middle school	Classroom binder
	Subject area	ELA (2), social studies	ELA, social studies	Math, science, social studies	ELA, social studies, science
8	Modes	Support an opinion, support a solution, character sketch	Explain a cause, explain a process	Compare and contrast, explain a process, description	Business letter, user manual, explain a process
	Revision	Circling picture sentences, writing leads	Combining sentences, writing leads, closes	Writing leads, writing closes	Jot and blend
	Proofreading	Triads	Sentence Check Chart	Sentence Check Chart	Triads
	Publishing	Business partner	Nearby high school	Classroom binder	Business partner
	Subject area	ELA, social studies	Math, science, social studies	ELA, social studies, science	Science, social studies, math

Appendix for Student Self-Assessment

The conscientious work of Rick Stiggins and the Assessment Training Institute (ATI) team of the Educational Testing Service (ETS) has informed our understanding of the power of student self-assessment. While student self-assessment appears in each chapter, this appendix accentuates the need for simple, consistent and pervasive student self-assessment. Feel free to adjust the expectations for each level of student performance upward; I have yet to meet a classroom of students that needed these expectations lowered. Increased expectations lead to accelerated student performance.

Chapter	Instructional Tool or Strategy	Expectations		
		▭	◎	+
6	Assignment Page	2–3 sentences	4–5 sentences	6 insightful sentences
7	Word bank	Fills roughly 50% of lines with vivid word choices	Fills roughly 75% of lines with vivid word choices	Fills all lines with vivid word choices
8	Framed Draft	Adds an average of 2–3 words per blank	Adds an average of 3–5 words per blank	Elaborately adds 5+ words per blank
9	Jot and Blend revision strategy	Blends an average of 1–2 words per sentence; numerous picture killers	Blends an average of 2–3 words per sentence; few picture killers	Blends an average of 3+ vivid words per sentence; minimal picture killers
10	Writing leads revision strategy	Writes two leads; may be repetitious and/or formulaic	Writes two distinctly developed leads; one hooks the attention of an audience	Writes two or more distinctly developed leads; two hook the audience's attention
	Writing closes revision strategy	Writes two closes; may be repetitious and/or formulaic	Writes two distinctly written closes; one provides closure or moves the audience to act or change	Writes two or more distinctly written closes; two provide closure or move the audience to act or change

Chapter	Instrucitonal Tool or Strategy	Expectations		
		▭	◎	+
11	Combining sentences revision strategy	Combines 1–2 pairs of sentences	Combines 3–4 two- and three-sentence groups	Combines 4+ two- and three-sentence groups; rewords for clarity
12	Proofing Strip	Corrects <50% of errors in triad	Corrects 50–75% of errors in triad	Corrects >75% of errors in triad
12	Sentence Check Chart proofreading strategy	Replaces half the beginning words and corrects <50% of errors in 16 sentences	Vividly replaces half of the beginning words and corrects 50–75% of errors in 16 sentences	Vividly replaces half the beginning words and corrects >75% of errors in 16 sentences
13	Final Evaluation Rubric	Minimally completes peer/self-evaluation. Little resemblance to teacher evaluation	Completes peer/self-evaluation that reflects understanding of stated standards	Insightfully completes peer/self-evaluation with comments added to those provided in the rubric
14	Unassisted Writing Sample	Writes throughout both sessions with a converted score of 70–80%	Writes throughout both sessions with a converted score of 80–90%	Writes throughout both sessions with a converted score of >90%
15	Publication strategy and place	Minimally completes a publication strategy	Exemplarily completes a publication strategy	Completes a publication strategy with novelty or creativity
6–15	Peer-Assisted Learning System Strategies	Coaches PALs with hesitation or confusion	Coaches PALs as directed	Coaches PALs with initiative
6–15	Author's Chair	Presents writing task and/or responds with reluctance	Presents writing task and/or responds without hesitation	Presents writing task and/or responds with proficiency

Appendix for PALS Strategies

Peer-**A**ssisted **L**earning **S**ystem (PALS): Research in teaching and learning concludes that students learn best from one another in classrooms when

- Teachers prompt students to interact with each other with concrete, specific expectations
- Students document in writing that they have followed their teachers' expectations

PALS strategies are embedded throughout the steps of a Writing Cycle. They work well in pairs or small groups of students in Author's Chair at the end of a day's work session. They also function in both small and large groups of students to bring closure to the week's writing tasks. They help pairs of students as they apply know-about knowledge of the Common Core State Standards in work sessions. In the following table, PAL A is an individual student, but PAL B can refer to one or more students, as teachers deem appropriate.

The PALS Routine for a Writing Cycle Framework

Strategy	PAL A	PAL B	PAL A
General		PAL B responds with directed routine.	PAL A records the response of PAL B in own writing
A Voice (style), **pictures** (ideas), **flow** (organization)		PAL B declares that the voice, pictures or flow in PAL A's writing is most noticeable and identifies two phrases as evidence.	PAL A circles the phrases and labels them with voice, pictures or flow.
B Accurate, complete or **accurate *and* complete**		PAL B points to evidence that language of a standard is 1) accurate: shows understanding of terms used 2) complete: uses all essential terms 3) accurate and complete: shows understanding of all terms of the standard	PAL A writes the words *accurate, complete* or *accurate and complete* on own writing.
C Logical, complete or **logical and complete**		PAL B points to evidence that language of a standard is 1) logical: sound logic in what is explained 2) complete: includes all points of the standard 3) logical and complete: sound logic in explaining all points of the standard	PAL A writes the words *logical, complete* or *logical and complete* on own writing.
D Connection to-source, to-self (own experience), **to-world** (observations or current events)		PAL B points to evidence of PAL A's examples connecting 1) **to-source** book or other reference tool 2) **to-self** or personal experience 3) **to-world** observation of others or current events	PAL A circles the examples that PAL B identifies and labels them 1) "text-to-source," 2) "text-to-self" or 3) "text-to-world."
E Appeal: data (statistics, facts); **logic** (deduction); **emotional** (beliefs)		PAL B points to evidence PAL A's examples appealed to 1) data, reports, quotations, records 2) logic, deduction, reasoning, analysis 3) emotion, beliefs, values, morals, principles, fears	PAL A circles the examples that PAL B identifies and labels them 1) data, 2) logic or 3) emotional.

PAL A reads his/her writing aloud verbatim to PAL B. (spanning the PAL A column)

References

Atwell, Nancie   2002 *Lessons that Change Writers*. Portsmouth, NH: Heinemann

Atwell presents carefully crafted lessons that take teachers and students through a definitive presentation of the writer's workshop model powered by student-teacher conferences (6–8).

1998 *In the Middle: New Understandings about Writing*. Portsmouth, NH: Boynton-Cook Publishers, Inc.

The second edition of this title, Atwell establishes the writer's workshop model for the middle grades (4–8). The most complete professional text of its kind, it provides extensive evidence of the validity of the workshop model in a myriad of student exemplars. It does not connect its practices to student performance on summative assessments of written expression.

Calkins, Lucy   The most read undergraduate text on the teaching of writing for K–8 students, *The Art of Teaching Writing* has done more to popularize the writer's workshop model than any other title. Its companion series, *First Hand: Units of study* for grades K–2 and 3–5 provides a full writing curriculum for the teaching of writing support by student exemplars of writing. Although her lessons move the teaching of writing into science, math and social studies, she offers no connection for them to student scores on tests of written expression.

Cazden, Courtney   The first educator to build on the theories of Noam Chomsky, Cazden released this readable graduate text for teachers of writing. While it does not embrace one mode of instruction over another, it was establish the theoretical and practice case that students learn the best by doing (*knowing-how*), then reflecting to understand what they have done (*knowing-that*).

Chomsky, Noam   1957 *Syntactic Structures*. The Hague, Netherlands: Mouton & Company.

Syntactic Structures was the first language study that attempted to construct a true scientific theory of a subject like the study of chemistry, mathematics or biology. It offers the *Language Acquisition Device* (*LAD*) that explains the pre-wired internal apparatus in all human brains that account for language learning. He also established the separate of grammar and meaning, citing "Colorless green ideas sleep furiously" as grammatical without meaning. Chomsky's later transformational-generative grammar is the system on which the sentence-combining language strategy is based. *Sentence Building* presents a full research-based curriculum based on sentence-combining practice.

Combs, Warren   2011 *A Writing Cycle for Writer's Workshop, K–2, 3–5, 6–8 and 9–12*. 4th ed. Athens, GA: Erincort Consulting, Inc.

A framework for delivering a standards-based approach to teaching the writing process and using writing to learn across the curriculum. Emphasis on multi-paragraph writing, including the written component of research projects.

A rich variety of critical-thinking strategies for short writing presented in a routine that captures the power of student self-assessment. A standards-based approach to writing to learn across the curriculum (6–12).

2011 *Sentence Building.* 3rd Ed, Athens, GA: Erincort Consulting, Inc.

A full presentation of sentence-combing exercises, the language strategy that posts the greatest Effect Size (ES) on improving writing from the writing intervention research for all three tiers of *Results through Intervention,* RtI (1–9).

2010 *Empowering Students to Write and RE-Write.* Larchmont, NY: Eye On Education.

In a companion text of professional development for middle and secondary teachers, Combs focuses on a wide variety of revision strategies for writing in all content areas of the 6–12 curricula. It features downloadable instructional tools and a guide for professional learning communities interested in studying the book together.

Council of Chief State Schools Officers 2010 *Common Core State Standards Initiative: Preparing America's Students for College and Career*

The publication of national task force for develop Common Core State Standards define what students should understand and be able to do by the end of each grade, grades K–12. It's most notable feature is the combining of all subjects of study under the English Language arts with the exception of mathematics. In spirit, the common core supports the workshop model for instruction with encouragement that each state determine the tools and strategies for helping students meet and exceed the stated standards in the use of the model.

Graham, Steve and Delores Perin (Ed.) 2007 *Writing Next.* Washington, DC: Alliance for Excellent Education

This most readable presentation of research in the teaching of writing reviews over 150 research studies of strategies in the teaching of writing. It limited its review to double-blind studies, the most valid experimental design. The data included lends strong credibility to prepared instructional tools used in *Writer's Workshop for the Common Core,* especially prewriting tools and revision strategies.

Graves, Donald The eternal optimist, Donald Graves is the author of the "quick writes" approach to launching writer's workshop. His influence on teachers of the *National Writing Project* surpasses estimation. An obvious influence on my approach to teaching writing, he admittedly focused on personal authorship of personal ideas as opposed to writing to learn state standards. Chapter 8, "Take Energy from Assessment," however, shows teachers of writer's workshop how to connect the model to student performance on tests of written expression.

Heard, Georgia 2002 *The Revision Toolbox: revision techniques that work.* Portsmouth, NH: Heinemann.

A readable presentation of instructional tools for teachers versed in teaching the writer's workshop model (3–8).

Marzano, Robert and Debra J. Pickering 2004 *Building Academic Vocabulary.* Alexandria, VA: Association of Supervision and Curriculum Development (ASCD).

This practical word study guide presents a six-step process in the instruction of vocabulary for use in whole- group, small-group or independent learning venues. It focuses on learning vocabulary in the context of the curriculum, particularly word families. It presents word study recommended for students on days when the teacher tutors small groups to bring them up to pace in the weekly pacing of a Writing Cycle.

Murray, Donald 1991 *The Craft of Revision.* New York, NY: Holt, Rinehart and Winston.

Foundational work for teaching students to revise. Award-winning journalist, professor and writing coach (6–college)

Noguchi, Rei 1991 *Grammar and the Teaching of Writing.* Urbana, IL: National Council of Teachers of English. See Chapter 11.

A comprehensive review of the teaching of grammar of American English from its beginning. Clearly establishes the negative effect of instruction in formal grammar on the quality of student writing. Cites sentence-combining practice as the model for teaching grammar that effects writing positively (K–college).

Reaves, Douglas 2006 *The Learning Leader.* Alexandria, VA: Association for Supervision and Curriculum Development.

One of Reaves' books that presents the research of the 90-90-90 schools. Establishes frequent writing as the common instructional strategy that posted the greatest gains in achievement and equity across the curriculum (K–12)

Saddler, Bruce and Steve Graham Although PALS is applied to the teaching of reading by others, Saddler and Graham are the first to use it in the context of teaching writing, specifically the study of language skills using sentence-combining practice. The application to author's chair in writer's workshop is pertinent and obvious.

Sousa, David 1995 *How the Brain Learns: A Classroom Teacher's Guide,* Reston, VA: National Association of Secondary School Principals.

Sousa pointedly emphasizes that all teaching is not directed towards students' brains, that certain teaching strategies and styles present new knowledge in ways that lack meaning for students. The book is a balance of theory and concrete practice that applies to all subjects and grade levels.

Stiggins, Richard 2003 *Classroom Assessment for Student Learning.* Princeton, NJ: Educational Testing Services

The definitive course on formative classroom assessment. The rationale and research findings that establish student self-assessment as the assessment that best improves student performance across the curriculum (K–12).

Correlation of *Writer's Workshop for the Common Core* to the Common Core State Standards

College and Career Readiness Anchor Standards for Writing, Language, Speaking, and Listening	Section of *Writer's Workshop for the Common Core*
Text Types and Purposes. 1. Write arguments to support claims in an analysis of substantive topics or texts, using valid reasoning and relevant and sufficient evidence.	Chapter 9
Text Types and Purposes. 2. Write informative/explanatory texts to examine and convey complex ideas and information clearly and accurately through the effective selection, organization and analysis of content.	Chapters 6, 7, 8, 9
Text Types and Purposes. 3. Write narratives to develop real or imagined experiences or events using effective technique, well-chosen details and well-structured event sequences.	Chapter 8
Production and Distribution of Writing. 4. Produce clear and coherent writing in which the development, organization and style are appropriate to task, purpose and audience.	Chapter 6
Production and Distribution of Writing. 5. Develop and strengthen writing as needed by planning, revising, editing, rewriting or trying a new approach.	Chapters 7, 8, 9, 10, 11, 12
Production and Distribution of Writing. 6. Use technology, including the Internet, to produce and publish writing and to interact and collaborate with others.	Chapter 15
Range of Writing. 10. Write routinely over extended time frames (time for research, reflection and revision) and shorter time frames (a single sitting or a day or two) for a range of tasks, purposes and audiences.	Chapters 3, 14, 15
Vocabulary Acquisition and Use. 4. Determine or clarify the meaning of unknown and multiple-meaning words and phrases by using context clues, analyzing meaningful word parts and consulting general and specialized reference materials, as appropriate.	Chapters 5–7
Vocabulary Acquisition and Use. 5. Demonstrate understanding of figurative language, word relationships and nuances in word meanings.	Chapters 5–7
Vocabulary Acquisition and Use. 6. Acquire and use accurately grade-appropriate general academic and domain-specific words and phrases, including those that signal contrast, addition and other logical relationships (e.g., however, although, nevertheless, similarly, moreover, in addition).	Chapter 11
Conventions of Standard English. 1. Demonstrate command of the conventions of standard English grammar and usage when writing or speaking.	Chapter 11
Conventions of Standard English. 2. Demonstrate command of the conventions of standard English capitalization, punctuation and spelling when speaking and writing.	Chapter 11
Comprehension and Collaboration. 1. Prepare for and participate effectively in a range of conversations and collaborations building on others' ideas and expressing their own clearly and persuasively.	Chapter 13